Acknowledgments and Thanks

Many thanks to my God and my family for support
and love beyond measure.

For Sara, my dear wife,
whom I love and fight for.

And to my children.

SUNRISE REFLECTIONS

FINDING HOPE IN HARD TIMES

A DEVOTIONAL

Skip
Coryell

Published by White Feather Press. (www.whitefeatherpress. com)

ISBN 978-1-61808-206-0
Cover design created by Ron Bell of AdVision Design Group (www.advisiondesigngroup.com)

White Feather Press

Reaffirming Faith in God, Family, and Country!

Books by Skip Coryell

We Hold These Truths
Bond of Unseen Blood
Church and State
Blood in the Streets
Laughter and Tears
RKBA: Defending the Right to Keep and Bear Arms
Stalking Natalie
The God Virus
The Shadow Militia
The Saracen Tide
The Blind Man's Rage
Civilian Combat - The Concealed Carry Book
Jackpine Strong
Concealed Carry for Christians
The Covid Chronicles: Surviving the Upgrade
The Covid Chronicles: Surviving the Apocalypse
The Covid Chronicles: Surviving the Solstice
The Mad American - Judgment Day
Sunrise Reflections: Finding Hope in Hard Times

Introduction

The great joy of life is to have a hope in something greater than ourselves as we face the future. All of us can survive without food and water for a season, but hope is the one thing that we can't live without for a moment, however we define it. Such hope is what makes us human and defines how we will face each day amidst the trials of life.

That is why this series of devotionals on hope entitled "Sunrise Reflections" is such a gift to read, meditate on and share with others. For Skip Coryell, these devotionals are the needed medicine for the soul we all need in this hour. Our world is facing what seem to be unprecedented levels of confusion and chaos all around us like never before. Multitudes of people are gripped with fear and anxiety as each new day arrives with yet another unfolding narrative of new drama to face. Discovering and being guided to real hope is the one thing that can calm those fears like nothing else and restore life to being the gracious gift it was meant to be.

As you read each devotional thought in this collection, Skip's steadfast source of hope is always centered and grounded in the Lord. When our hearts begins to focus on the hope only the Lord can give things will somehow change right away. We will begin to be joyfully led out of our small worlds into the Lord's big world. In that world, things don't end with us and our problems, but rather they begin with the Lord and His solutions. Making that transition from ourselves to the Lord is the great challenge we always face. That is why "Sunrise Reflections" can be such a wonderful tool to nudge us forward to a new place of hope each day.

Skip's devotionals on hope are a relevant and helpful resource for everyone, no matter who we are or what our backgrounds might be. They will speak to the mature Christian, as well as to the seeker looking for a place to begin their spiritual journey. The style of these devotionals is easy to read, thoughtful, humorous at times and filled with stories and quotes to make each one a rich experience to enjoy, celebrate and share with others. I think you will find them memorable and a source of inspiration.

As Skip's pastor and friend I know that this book is something that Skip has personally lived himself and delights in sharing with others. Skip is the real deal and his honesty and authenticity will jump out at you. These devotionals reflect the deepest sense of a Christian on a journey of discovery to get through the hardest challenges of life in this hour and end at the finish line of hope in the arms of the Lord. So I invite you to join Skip on this journey. It is a journey worth taking. I believe the Lord will use these devotionals to bless you and give you the hope we all need each day.

Pastor Jeff Carlson
Oakhill Church
Grand Rapids, Michigan
Summer 2021

Foreword

Please note in Jesus' first podcast, The Sermon on the Mount, the following three observations:

1. Jesus promised pain.
2. Not everyone's going to make it.
3. His preaching had a punch.

It's crystal clear, at least to me, that Jesus promised pain. He doesn't say if you get hit by a storm, but when you get hit by a storm.

In contrast to Christ's clear teaching regarding the promise of pain in this life, we have our current crop of ear-tickilin' ... butt-kissin' effeminate ministers who lie to believers telling them once they say 'yes to Jesus', life will become an uninterrupted lite beer commercial of trouble-free living, one of non-stop pixie dust and candy canes.

Jesus nuked that heretical notion in His first sermon.

Everyone gets a storm.

Everyone will have bad things happen to them.

What's refreshing about this promise of pain is:

It's nonsense free. Jesus forewarns folks of impending, could be calamitous, trials heading towards everyone who strolls this terra firma and they could be devastating if you've been playing games in a Christian Disneyland, not erecting your life on His eternal principles.

This shock-and-awe, reality-based revelation, laid to the psyche of those who have ears to hear causes them to prepare accordingly and build their lives well. Forewarning equals forearming to the shrewd follower of the Galilean. Here Jesus is being a drill sergeant slapping His troops around and getting them ready to rumble in a spiritual war that's about to hit them in the kisser.

Indeed, in our times we give participation 'trophies' to clods who rocked up in 9th Place or ran the wrong way in a relay race.

Not so with Jesus.

He gives it to the crowd straight: The storms/tests are coming and they will reveal whether or not we have built according to His word. If we have, then we'll be fine. If we haven't, well ... don't blame God or your mommy ... or anybody else. Blame yourself.

It's clear, and Skip addresses it right off the bat, in this fresh devotional, that we're in dire straits as a country. Stevie Wonder can see that. The storms aren't coming. They're here, in full measure. Indeed, if 'something' isn't done by freedom-loving patriotic Christians, then this grand experiment in self-governance will vanish like a pack of smokes at an AA meeting.

If we truly wish to 'fix' what's jacked up about our country we've got to do this thing called 'repent'. Honestly, and I know I'm going to sound like a snake-handling pentecostal, if we, as a people, don't beat a serious path back to a right relationship with God, through Jesus Christ, then we, as a nation, are doomed to collapse.

And that's what I dig about Skip's book. In the midst of cataclysmic lies that are rocking our world comes the simple clarion call to worship Christ, focus on the family, and cherish our hard-won freedoms. You may think that's a childish recipe for such an abysmal mess but it is exactly what Jesus said would cause a person and a nation to stand when others fall.

Doug Giles
Clashdaily.com
Author, *Rules for Radical Christians*

From the author

Summer, 2021

I love to watch the movie *The Hunger Games*; it stars Jennifer Lawrence as the heroic Katniss Everdeen and Donald Sutherland as the evil President Snow. One quote from that movie gives us a lot of insight into life, especially now, as we face hard times.

> *"Hope, it is the only thing stronger than fear. A little hope is effective, a lot of hope is dangerous. A spark is fine, as long as it's contained."*

> *– President Snow, The Hunger Games*

Right now, all across the world, many people are losing hope. It is being replaced by fear. Fear of the unknown. Fear of poverty. Fear of global pandemic. Fear of death and violence. Fear of turmoil and social upheaval.

We are in the middle of transition, and change frightens people. President Snow was a fictitious character, but he represents real tyrants out there who are eager to extinguish all hope from the world. And all tyrants work for Satan, the ultimate tyrant.

My primary purpose for writing this book is to rekindle hope within the hearts and minds of humanity, especially my fellow Christians, because we are the ones who harbor the ultimate hope of the universe. But here's the thing, the President Snows of this world cannot defeat us unless we first surrender.

Every day I have to remind myself that God is in control, no matter how bleak it may look in the news. Lately,

I've been spending less time in the news and more time in the Bible; less time talking about politics and more time talking to God.

There is no doubt that the world is coming upon hard times, dark times ... times where President Snow would snuff out the tiny spark of hope that we guard within the privacy of our own hearts. But each day I struggle to remember who I am in Christ, of His promises, of His love, and of His power.

In reality, the battle belongs to the Lord, and the only way we can be defeated is by giving up. Surrender and despair is of the evil one. He wants you to give up, because it's the only way he can win. He will isolate you, discourage you, and try to render you impotent. But don't fall for that. Every new sunrise is a reminder of God's power and love for His creation. So hold on to the promise that every new sunrise represents.

God loves you. And He will be with you always ... even to the end of the age. And the Son has already risen!

– Skip Coryell

sagacity
[suh-gas-i-tee]

noun
acuteness of mental discernment
and soundness of judgment.
dictionary.com

> "...when sagacity is able to perceive
> the beneficialness, then faith cannot
> see God; but when in the dark night
> of suffering sagacity cannot see a
> handbreadth ahead of it, then faith
> can see God, since faith sees best in
> the dark."
>
> – Søren Kierkegaard

*11 Now faith is confidence in what we
hope for and assurance about what we
do not see. 2 This is what the ancients
were commended for. 3 By faith we understand that the universe was formed
at God's command, so that what is seen
was not made out of what was visible.*

Hebrews 11:1-3 (NIV)

THEY CALL ME
JUNGLE BUTT

T WAS BACK IN **1976,** AND I WAS
with a battalion of Marines in the jungles of Panama
on a training exercise. The training was really quite
simple: Force march all day long up the muddy slopes all
the while trying not to fall down or grab onto those terrible thorny Black Palm trees. I remember it would rain
for a half hour until we shivered in 100 percent humid-
ity and ninety-degree heat. Then we'd pray for the sun to
come out, and then it would bake us in the steam until we
prayed for the rain to return and cool us off again. After a
few days we were all a soggy, miserable mess. To top it all
off, all night long, while we were supposed to be sleeping,
the not-so-friendly, neighborhood Green Berets would
continually probe our defensive perimeter, looking for
gaps and lobbing in bomb simulators (more bomb than
simulator I think).

In all honesty, I have never seen such a thick and heavy
darkness. On those black nights, I recall holding my hand
up in front of my face and being surprised that I couldn't

1

see it. It was just a few inches away, and I knew it was there, but I just had no sensory evidentiary support.

I recall one afternoon they stuck me on a listening post about a mile out with a PRC 77 radio on my back. I was a lowly private at the time, and took to my mission with a vengeance. I found this strange jungle plant growing up about five feet tall with palm fronds extending out three-hundred and sixty degrees all around. It gave me perfect concealment, so I nestled down inside it and waited for the Green Berets to happen by. They never came. Instead, my behind started to itch and burn. I scratched the itch and the itching got worse. After only a half hour on post, I couldn't stand it any longer. I was only eighteen at the time, and I recall thinking "What if this stuff is poisonous? Am I going to die?"

I remembered the Captain's orders, "Only use the radio when you make enemy contact or in extreme emergencies." The more I scratched my backside, the more it itched and burned. I quickly concluded that this was indeed a dire emergency. I fired up the radio and called into battalion HQ requesting a helicopter come in and medevac me out of the jungle. I was appalled at the Captain's lack of empathy. Not only did he refuse to send a helicopter, but he ordered me to get off the radio and tough it out until nightfall.

Long story short, the Captain was right. I survived and the itching went away after about four hours. But after that my new unofficial call sign was known as "Jungle Butt."

The moral of the story?

SOMETIMES IN LIFE THINGS HAPPEN TO US THAT

make us feel like we're trapped inside the jungle. I don't know if you've ever been in the jungle, but the jungle has a thick canopy overhead, and, at night, you sometimes can't see the stars. You know they must be up there, but you just can't see them. I remember times like that in my life where all seemed lost. I couldn't see the stars. I couldn't see the moon. I couldn't see the sun. All seemed hopelessly lost.

In times like that, when all seems hopelessly lost, when there is no visible light at the end of the tunnel, when people all around us are giving in to despair; those are the times when we must remain upbeat and positive. Because, in reality, hope is never hopelessly lost. There is always hope, and there is always God who loves us and cares for us; who watches out for us; who is always walking beside us even though we can't visibly see Him.

"I believe in Christianity as I believe that the sun has risen: not only because I see it, but because by it I see everything else."

— *C.S. Lewis*

"To one who has faith, no explanation is necessary. To one without faith, no explanation is possible."

— *Thomas Aquinas*

"Faith sees the invisible, believes the unbelievable, and receives the impossible."

— *Corrie Ten Boom*

When all is said and done, what you can see with your eyes is just a small part of life. Faith is a choice. Choose to believe ... to hope ... and peace will follow.

The Bible reminds us that God is always there for us. Never lose hope; no matter what happens in your life. God is always there. God always loves you. The world will let you down, but God is always there for you. Remember God's promise to Joshua? He has the same promise for you.

weed
[weed]

noun
1. a valueless plant growing wild, especially one that grows on cultivated
ground to the exclusion or injury of
the desired crop.
2. any undesirable or troublesome
plant, especially one that grows pro-
fusely where it is not wanted:

dictionary.com

He has made everything beautiful in its time. He has also set eternity in the human heart; yet no one can fathom what God has done from beginning to end.

Ecclesiastes 3:11 (NIV)

THESSA WITH FLOWERS

THE BOND BETWEEN A **10**-YEAR-old little girl and her father is a special one. My little girl's name is Amethyst, but here around the house we just call her Thessa for short.

Amethyst's passion in life is the search for and the love of all things beautiful. To quote Stephen R. Donaldson, New York Times best-selling fantasy author, "Something there is ... in beauty." And to me, Thessa is the most beautiful little girl on the planet.

Thessa and I do many wonderful things together. Sometimes we take a walk around our very large yard and look for flowers. Right about now in mid-July we don't have to look very hard, because they're all over the place. I'm amazed at the simplicity of her spirit. As a young girl she can get excited over the most basic of things. Take dandelions for instance. To us adults they are a nuisance, but not to little Thessa. To her they are a wonder to behold, something to be treasured, to be picked and cuddled, to be placed in a cup of water and given to her mother as a most treasured gift and accompanied by a hug and a kiss..

To little Thessa, the simple things that us adults take for granted are wonderful and grandiose. So many times us adults get caught up in the rat race of society, its problems, its ills, its downright corruption, and then ... we lose our ability to recognize and revere God's beautiful creation. God made it all for us you know. To make it more personal, almighty God, the creator of the universe (a very important person by the way) He made the sun, the moon, the stars and all those pretty little flowers so that you could look at them in awe and see a reflection of who God really is.

God is amazing. And God is beautiful too.

Thessa's love of nature isn't restricted to flowers; it also extends to what us adults call *weeds*. But to Amethyst, anything with a blossom is a flower ... a beautiful treasure to be held and admired.

I believe God looks at all of us that way, just like Thessa does. Because, let's face it, some of us aren't all that beautiful. Sometimes, by virtue of our poor behavior, us adults can act downright ugly. We fall into sin, and then we no longer feel like beautiful blossoms created by God, but more like weeds that need to be pulled and composted.

And here's the kicker. Amethyst wants to please me. She loves me and reveres me even more than she does her flowers. And that is a most precious opportunity. But the opportunity comes with a time limit. Because I do not own Thessa; she is a child of God just like me.

One of my greatest fears is that I'll let her down; that I'll screw up and make her ashamed of me; that I'll prove myself unworthy of her love. As her father, God has tasked me with a near-impossible feat: to show Amethyst just a tiny glimpse of who God is. I am a vague picture of God our heavenly father, a grainy, out of focus tintype. But herein lies my hope: that I'll follow Christ closely enough so that Thessa will recognize God in me and realize just how much He loves her.

I am Thessa's father. She thinks I'm beautiful. And just this one time ... I'm not going to correct her.

The moral of the story?

As a father my job is to raise up God's children, to love them, to nurture them, to protect them from all harm both physical and spiritual. My own father could sometimes be harsh and cruel, and as a result, I grew up to believe God was standing over me, waiting for me to make a mistake so He could punish me. It took me decades to figure out who God really was, how much He loved me and treasured me.

While growing up, I was convinced I was nothing but a weed, of no great value; just a nuisance to be pulled up and cast into the fire. Ironically, it was my little girl who helped me overcome that. She loved me and helped me feel my true value before God.

You are not a weed, but a child of God. As you go through your day, try to remember that to God you are a beautiful flower, to be loved, revered and cuddled. So when Satan whispers in your ear that you are nothing but a weed, just smile and tell him to get behind you.

I am a child of God, a beautiful flower ... and He loves me.

"God writes the gospel not in the Bible alone, but on trees and flowers and clouds and stars."

— *Martin Luther*

"Never lose an opportunity of seeing anything beautiful, for beauty is God's handwriting."

— *Ralph Waldo Emerson*

"We delight in the beauty of the butterfly, but rarely admit the changes it has gone through to achieve that beauty."

— *Maya Angelou*

When all is said and done, a little girl is God's gift to her father. She reminds her dad that life is precious, that beauty exists, no matter how tough it gets to pay the bills, and no matter how mean your boss is at work. She loves you even when the garbage disposal breaks and you don't know how to fix it.

The little girl is your gift, a reminder that God loves you and that you are not a weed. You are a beautiful flower.

And something there is ... in beauty!

tomorrow
[tuh-mawr-oh]

noun
1. the day following today:

2. a future period or time:

From the rising of the sun to the place
where it sets, the name of the Lord is
to be praised.

Psalm 113:3 (NIV)

A RED SUN RISES

SOMETHING PROFOUNDLY COM-
mon happened today. The sun came out. It's
not that I wasn't expecting it to happen. I
mean, really ... it came out yesterday too ... and the day
before that and the day before that. And I'll bet my bottom
dollar that it comes out tomorrow as well.

The sun is still on the rise as I write. It is a glowing red
orb this morning, but it's always different in some large or
small way. But I like them all ... all the sunrises.

The sun is a symbol of hope. It's God almighty, bend-
ing down to kiss the earth and say in his most tender and
fatherly voice. "See, I told you it would happen. There now,
I've given you another day, and I can't wait to see what
you're going to do with it!"

Last night I got a call from a friend of mine. It was a sad
call, telling me how much he loved his wife who had left
him after thirty-plus years. What do you say to a man who
is trapped deep within the bowels of night, who is facing
the long, dark night of his soul. He will not be happy again
for many months, perhaps even years.

I know from personal experience that tragedies like the

one happening to him leave a wound that may never totally heal. It reminds me of a conversation in JRR Tolkein's *Fellowship of the Ring* between Gandalf the wizard and Lord Elrond the elf.

Elrond: His strength returns.

Gandalf: That wound will never fully heal. He will carry it the rest of his life.

Elrond: And yet, to have come so far, still bearing the Ring, the hobbit has shown extraordinary resilience to its evil.

Gandalf: It is a burden he should never have had to bear. We can ask no more of Frodo.

So what do you tell a friend whose world has just imploded unexpectedly? Many people have no frame of reference, so they say something trite for lack of anything better. They promise to pray, and sometimes they do, but many times not ... if we're really honest about it.

When my friend called, I didn't want to be trite or simplistic. I wanted to say something that might help him make it through this dark time in his life. But I don't always know the right thing to say. In fact, most often times I don't. In times like that I try to keep my mouth shut and just listen. I find it difficult to experience someone in pain, simply because I know what they're going through and the remembrance brings me pain as well.

Author M Scott Peck once wrote that "A wise man welcomes pain and sees it as a way to grow." Even though he's right, that's not the thing to say to a grieving husband who's just lost the love of his life. Later on he'll be able to understand and appreciate that wisdom, but not right now.

Just like Frodo the hobbit, my friend has just been stabbed in the heart by an evil Morgul blade, and he will carry the wound forever. There will be a scar and a tender spot for the rest of his life here on earth.

The moral of the story?

I'm reminded of Job's three friends (Eliphaz, Bildad and Zophar) who were really no help at all. I didn't want to be like Job's friends. And I thought to myself "What is the most important thing I can give my friend right now? What does he need most?"

The answer that came back to me was simple. He needs the sunrise, the hope of a new day, a better time. Think about it. Why do people take their own lives? The answer is simple. They take their own lives when they lose hope, when they can't see beyond their own pain and they start believing that this pain will last forever. That message is a deadly lie. Here is what I told my friend.

Everything with a beginning has an end. Your pain will not last forever. The road will be long and dark, but you are not on the road alone. God is with you, holding your hand, giving you hugs, living and feeling the pain right along with you.

The pain will slowly subside and one day you'll come out the other side and see the sunrise in all its beauty. If you're going through a hard time, the best thing you can do is stay as close to God as you can. God will never give you a burden too great for you to bear. And He will bear it with you. God will never leave you.

"There was never a night or a problem that could defeat sunrise or hope."

– Bernard Williams

"Get outside. Watch the sunrise. Watch the sunset. How does that make you feel? Does it make you feel big or tiny? Because there's something good about feeling both."

– Amy Grant

The sun will come out Tomorrow

So ya gotta hang on 'Til tomorrow

Come what may."

–'Tomorrow' From the musical "Annie" lyrics by Martin Charnin

When all is said and done, I guarantee you the sun will come out tomorrow. So, I encourage you most ardently to hang on till tomorrow.

Each new day brings with it a new sunrise, a new beginning, a new hope, and a second chance.

Claim today's sunrise for your own. Make it your own personal second chance. Because God has created today's brand new sun just for you, and He waits now with baited breath, cheering you on and asking ... "What wonderful thing will you do with this new day I've given you?"

purpose
[pur-puhs]

noun
1. the reason for which something
exists or is done, made, used, etc.

dictionary.com

Many are the plans in a person's heart, but it is the Lord's purpose that prevails.

Proverbs 19:21 (NIV)

MY PLACE
IN THIS WORLD

ONE OF MY FAVORITE MODERN, Christian artists is Michael W Smith. His songs and sounds move me to reflection, to purpose and to greater service. My all-time favorite of his songs is titled *Place in this World*.

The secular view of purpose in life is much different than for those who serve Christ. In the secular world it's all about what is best for the individual, what will make you happy, what do you enjoy, what are you passionate about? It's all about self.

But the Christian view on life's purpose is much different. In God, we live and move and have our being. It's not all about us. There's a fried chicken franchise that used to print the following words on all their buckets of chicken. "One life 'twill soon be passed; only what's done for Christ will last."

And that is so true. Throughout my teens and twenties I struggled to find my place in this world. The struggle brought me down many false trails and a few times I lost my way. In the end I did discover my place in this world, but it wasn't what I expected it to be. Because my place in this world isn't even in this world. That's a trick, a lie, a distraction that takes us down a rabbit hole of no return.

Many people spend their whole lives inside the rabbit hole and never really figure it out. In the end, here's what I discovered.

There are only two questions in life that I have to answer.

1. Who is my master?
2. How can I best serve Him?

As a young man I tried to complicate life. I studied philosophy, all the great minds that humanity had to offer, but, in the end, all man's wisdom turned out to be folly.

In the end, after great pain and cogitation, I discovered that God is my master. He is my creator and I live and breathe only by virtue of His love for me.

In 1979 Bob Dylan sang these words:

But you're gonna have to serve somebody, yes indeed
You're gonna have to serve somebody
Well, it may be the devil or it may be the Lord
But you're gonna have to serve somebody

Satan understands this truth as well. He knows you will either serve him or God. He wants you to serve him and will go to great lengths to steer you in his direction.

In the end, I chose to serve God, but not before I spent a few years kicking against the goads and rebelling against God. I discovered that Satan always serves his best wine first, then, after that, payment comes due. And the price was more than I was willing to bear. After all, what good does it do to gain the whole world, but to lose your own soul? Answer? None at all. In answer to question 1: God is my Master.

That brings us to question 2. How can I best serve Him. That one's a bit tougher, because the details are different for everyone. The basics are the same though. we can best serve God by deciphering His will for our life and working every day to live out our purpose.

The moral of the story?

No person can serve two masters, and trying to do so is nothing short of spiritual contortionism. It will twist your life and your heart up in knots. If you want to be happy, to find peace, to have purpose and joy in your life, then God is the best master. Seek after Him with all your heart, soul and mind.

Will it always be easy? No. Sometimes it will be very difficult. Will it always be fun? No, not at all. But God never promised us easy fun. I think that was Satan's promise. And, of course, he lied.

"One life 'twill soon be passed; only what's done for Christ will last."

— Chicken Coop Fried Chicken

Lookin' for a reason
Roamin' through the night to find
My place in this world
My place in this world
Not a lot to lean on
I need your light to help me find
My place in this world
My place in this world

— Michael W Smith

When all is said and done, only one master remains. God is the one, true master for all of creation. You can waste your entire life chasing down rabbit holes, or you can cut to the chase and serve God almighty.

When I think of my teens and twenties, all that wasted time and effort trying to figure out my place in this world, I softly sigh and laugh at myself.

I could have saved a lot of time by finding the meaning of life written on a box of fried chicken.

home
[hohm]

noun
1. a house, apartment, or other shelter that is the usual residence of a person, family, or household.
2. the place in which one's domestic affections are centered.

dictionary.com

In my little town
I grew up believing
God keeps his eye on us all
And He used to lean upon me
As I pledged allegiance to the wall
Lord, I recall
My little town

– Simon & Garfunkel

When the Lord had finished speaking
with Abraham, he left, and Abraham
returned home.

– Genesis 18:33 (NIV)

THE MILL POND

EVERY PERSON ON THE PLANET IS born somewhere. We all have a home town. And along with that goes a certain amount of sentiment. I'm proud of my home town, and I have very fond memories and feelings for the people and the community. But it wasn't always so.

As a teen I wanted nothing more than to leave my home town and never look back. I was like Simon and Garfunkel in their song *My Little Town*. I thought if I couldn't get out of here then I'd die for sure. Like the lyrics to their song:

"Nothing but the dead and dying
Back in my little town."

Wow, did I screw up on that one! But I was young and impressionable, ready for excitement and I wanted to go out and conquer the world. It reminds me of George Bailey from one of my favorite movies *It's a Wonderful Life.*

"I'm shakin' the dust of this crummy little town
off my feet and I'm gonna see the world. Italy,

Greece, the Parthenon, the Colosseum."

I was such a smart boy at age 17. I knew it all, and what I didn't know was worth knowing. I had an authoritative, overbearing father and I wanted to get out from under his totalitarian thumb. So, in desperation I joined the Marine Corps. All you military veterans out there are laughing at me now, because you know what's coming.

I'm not saying the Marine Corps was a bad experience. In fact, it was a very good experience and it made me a better man. But I am saying that it was difficult. Here's the best way I can describe boot camp. "I'm really glad that I did it. But I'm equally glad that I'll never have to do it again."

After that I went off to college, got married, got divorced, got married, got divorced. (No, that's not a typo.) By this time I was so sick of the world that I missed my crummy, little town every waking moment of my life. But what I found was that once you leave your little town it's not always easy to find your way back.

Finally, on my third marriage, at age 58, I finally made it back to the teeny, tiny, little town of Orangeville. And I've never been this happy in my whole life. My life has come full circle, and now I spend my golden years in the same place where I spent my youth.

I'm parked in my truck now on the banks of the Mill Pond. That means nothing to anyone who didn't grow up here, but to us Orangevillians here in southwest Michigan it means that I've come home. It means peace and tranquility.

The Mill pond is small with a dam about six feet high. The water rushes down the dam into the lower mill race and then makes it's way into the Orangeville Creek.

I'm listening to the water right now, cascading over rocks, bouncing and flowing, always moving, never dead and dying. As a child I swam every week during summer in these cool, refreshing waters ... as did my father and his father before him.

And now, once again, I take my children to the Mill Pond to swim as I did. I look into the water now, the reflections, the foam floating along the surface, and I can't help but think: the water that I'm seeing right now will some day make its way to the ocean. It will flow into Orangeville Creek, then to the Gun River, to the Kalamazoo River, to Lake Michigan and out the St. Lawrence Seaway.

The moral of the story?

And now, after 64 years, I realize that this is all the world I need to see. So, in celebration, Toto and I will close our eyes, listen to the water, slowly tap our heels together three times, and whisper the age-old mantra:

There's no place like home.
There's no place like home.
There's no place like home.

When all is said and done, home is the place where you feel the peace and love of God. For most people that's the place of their birth, where they grew up and made their start in this world. So many people move away, searching for a better life, only to return in their old age, coming full circle ... coming home.

But here's the rub. As a Christian I understand that I'm only visiting this planet. Earth is a picture of a much better place. And that reminds me of another song by B. J. Thomas.

I'm going home, going home
Where I belong

While I'm here I'll serve Him gladly
And sing Him all my songs
I'm here, but not for long

And when I'm feeling lonely
And when I'm feeling blue
It's such a joy to know that
I am only passing through

I'm headed home, going home
Where I belong

— B. J. Thomas

pain
[peyn]

noun
1. physical suffering or distress, as
due to injury, illness, etc.
2. a distressing sensation in a particular part of the body:
a back pain.
3. mental or emotional suffering or
torment:

dictionary.com

My back is filled with searing pain;
there is no health in my body.

— Psalm 38:7 (NIV)

IT'S NOT THE YEARS
IT'S THE MILES

RENEE DESCARTES WAS A FAmous French philosopher, born in 1596, and died in 1650. Renee is the genius who figured out humans really exist. I'm just a country bumpkin from Orangeville, but I had that one figured out the first time my mom bared my butt and gave me a good spanking. People get famous for the oddest things.

Mr. Descartes is most famous for his saying "I think, therefore I am."

When I was a young man I used to ponder such nonsense, but not so much anymore. I just don't have time for it. I think it's pretty much a given that you and I really do exist. When I was in high school I would write every day in my diary; it was a green spiral notebook where I kept all my innermost musings. As I read back through it today, I can't help but think, *Wow, Skip. You really were quite stupid.*

I recall trying to figure out the meaning of life. I'd ask questions like: Does God exist? Am I really alive? What is my purpose in life?

And all those are good questions, but here's the deal. Some people go through their entire lives and never find the correct answer to those questions. For many years I tried to find the meaning of life using the trial-and-error method. That didn't work very well for me. In fact, it caused me a lot of pain.

There was a song written by two school teachers back in the 1970s. They tried to get it published, but it was rejected 20 times until a singer named Johnny Lee finally agreed to record it in 1980. The song was titled *Looking for Love*.

> *"Well I spent a lifetime looking for you*
> *Single bars and good time lovers were never*
> *true*
> *Playing a fool's game*
> *Hoping to win*
> *And telling those sweet lies and losing again."*

I think many people go their entire lives looking for answers to the universal questions in life, but never really find anything that satisfies them. In my own life, I did the same thing. My first two wives didn't work for me. Why? Because I was looking for love in the wrong place.

That old saying, *the third time's a charm* was true for me. It took me 25 years of trial and error and a multitude of pain, but I finally figured out that you don't look for love in a bar, just like you don't look for meaning and purpose in a secular world.

The third time I chose a woman who already knew the meaning to life: to serve God by loving those around her.

And now, in my Golden years, as I sit in my rocking chair on the deck, watching the grass grow and the birds chirp, I can't help but think, I could've saved a lot of time and pain if I'd just done it God's way the first time.

Buddha said that "All of life is suffering." I don't think

Buddha and I would get along very well, because I've had enough suffering and pain for one life.

The moral of the story?

Now that I'm 64 years old, I've taken Descarte's original thesis and modified it a bit. When I was in my prime, I'd wake up every morning, feeling good, feeling strong, ready to run, to fight, to work and play hard. My body was young and strong, and pretty much did whatever I told it to do.

Now, after a lifetime of broken bones, back injuries, separated shoulders, sprains, strains, twists and contusions, I have a different take on life.

This morning I woke up and I stretched, and the stretching caused me great pain. Why? Because I exist.

"I hurt, therefore I am."

Any twenty-something kid with half a brain can think. Thinking? That's easy, but living for 80-plus years until your body gives out and you milk it for all it's worth? Now, hey, that's an accomplishment.

Getting old isn't for the faint of heart. At age 64, I can honestly say that there isn't a moment in time where I don't feel "A distressing sensation in a particular part of my body."

Renee Descarte died at age 53. What did he know? He was just a baby.

My comfort in my suffering is this: Your promise preserves my life.

— Psalm 119:50 (NIV)

je pense, donc je suis (French)

Cogito, ergo sum (Latin)

I think therefore I am

— René Descartes

When all is said and done, much of life is suffering and pain. But there is a flip side to that coin as well. God gave us rules to live by, rules that limit our suffering and pain. Much of the pain in my own life was self-inflicted. I could have avoided it simply by following God's rules and seeking out His will for my life.

If I had it all to do over again, I would submit my life and heart to God from the start. I would fall to my knees and cry out in a loud voice:

"Here I am God, a sinner. I praise you and worship you. I am yours to command."

purity
[pyoor-i-tee]

noun
1. the condition or quality of being
pure; freedom from anything that de-
bases, contaminates, pollutes, etc.:

dictionary.com

firewall
[fahyuhr-wawl]

noun
1. a person, thing, or event that acts
as a barrier or protection against
something undesirable:

dictionary.com

How can a young person stay on the path of purity? By living according to your word.

– Psalm 119:9 (NIV)

FIREWALL

THE OTHER NIGHT MY WIFE AND I were watching a movie that we'd watched many years ago. And then we came to a scene that shocked me so much that I had to pause the show. I looked at Sara and said, "I don't remember that part being in there."

It was a scene with explicit content that was inappropriate for our children. We didn't remember it, because the last time we'd watched it our children were either very young or not in the room. I quickly fast-forwarded through the scene until it was appropriate again.

Later on, lying in bed, I got to thinking. How could I not remember that sexually explicit scene? It clearly was there, but I had no recollection of it. We've had to do that many times in the past five years or so, and we ended up throwing away a lot of our old movies. What I've come to realize, is that having children in the house helps to hold me accountable.

A child's mind is less warped and tainted, so they are particularly sensitive to immorality in all its forms. But I had to ask the question of myself: How did I become so desensitized to sin? In my mind I understand and believe that sex outside of marriage is wrong, but then I watch it happen on television without blinking an eye.

As a healthy, red-blooded male I find it difficult to make it through the day without being tempted. Sexual immorality is everywhere. It's on television, billboards, the internet. You can't get away from it, not when reading a book, working on the computer or even driving your car.

Our society has become so corrupt that we no longer recognize sin for what it really is. The prophet Isaiah talked about this:

"Woe to those who call evil good and good evil, who put darkness for light and light for darkness, who put bitter for sweet and sweet for bitter."

Isaiah 5:20 (NIV)

I see this every day in our culture now. People no longer know the difference between right and wrong. Their hearts are seared, and many no longer understand the need or possibility of living a life free from immorality.

I was raised in a very strict church that put an emphasis on separation and purity. I scoffed at them and thought them to be self-righteous and holier than thou. But later on in life, after I'd become immoral, then I understood the need to become clean. I learned that righteous living has its own reward built right in.

I really like the movie with Kirk Cameron called *Fireproof*. It speaks to this issue of purity, especially in men, and it really hits home.

When my son, Cedar, was five years old, we sent him to public school. He'd been there only a few weeks when my sweet, innocent little boy came home swearing like a drunken sailor. I said, "Son, where did you learn that?" His answer, "On the playground."

My wife and I made some major changes in our life. She quit her high-paying, engineering job and started home-schooling our kids. She's been doing that for 10 years now, and it's one of the best parenting decisions we've ever made.

Some of my relatives didn't like that we were doing that. They said our kids wouldn't be properly socialized staying home all the time. Here's how I responded. "Why would I want my children to be socialized by Sodom and Gomorrah?"

My children are in the world, but not of the world. God has called Christians to be different. He has set us apart for His special purpose.

The moral of the story?

Look at it this way. When you place a healthy apple inside a bushel of rotten fruit, what happens? The outcome is predictable. The healthy fruit will begin to rot.

Be careful what you see with your eyes and hear with your ears. You are not better than other people, but you are owned by God. If God wouldn't watch that movie or look at that billboard ... then neither should you.

consecrate
[kon-si-kreyt]

verb
1. to make or declare sacred; set apart or dedicate to the service of a deity:

dictionary.com

*9 I wrote to you in my letter not to asso-
ciate with sexually immoral people— 10
not at all meaning the people of this
world who are immoral, or the greedy
and swindlers, or idolaters. In that case
you would have to leave this world. 11
But now I am writing to you that you
must not associate with anyone who
claims to be a brother or sister but is
sexually immoral or greedy, an idolater
or slanderer, a drunkard or swindler. Do
not even eat with such people.*

— 1 Corinthians 5:9-11 (NIV)

When all is said and done, you are the firewall between the world and your kids. If you don't protect them and filter out the impurities, then they'll become polluted and desensitized to sin and they will succumb to its sickness.

You are the firewall and sin is the virus. You must live a Godly life to the best of your ability. You can't do it alone. Invite Godly people into your life and encourage them to hold you accountable.

Like a muddied spring or a polluted well are the righteous who give way to the wicked.

Proverbs 25:26 (NIV)

exercise
[ek-ser-sahyz]

noun
1. bodily or mental exertion, especially for the sake of training or im-
provement of health:

dictionary.com

torture
[tawr-cher]

noun
1. the act of inflicting excruciating
pain, as punishment or revenge, as
a means of getting a confession or
information, or for sheer cruelty

dictionary.com

*For physical training is of some value,
but godliness has value for all things,
holding promise for both the present
life and the life to come.*

– 1 Timothy 4:8 (NIV)

MARTIAL ART
MUNCHKINS

EXERCISE IS A DEMONIC FORM OF
torture straight from the pits of hell. Perhaps
that last statement caught you off guard.
Probably because you and I both know it's not true.
Nonetheless, I hate exercise, even though it's good for me.
Some people start out liking exercise, like running, aerobics, and weight lifting just to name a few. I've even heard
rumor of some weird thing called Zumba out there where
people dance around real fast trying to get their heart rate
up. I guess it's from South America somewhere, and a lot
of women just love it. It sounds painful to me. And I wonder ... what do they call a person who practices Zumba?
Are they zumba-ites? Or zumbies? If that's the case, then
I'm more of a zombie than a zumbie.

Now, don't get me wrong, I love being in shape, and I
think everyone should be in shape. I just don't like what it
takes to get there. Getting in shape takes time, effort, sweat
and pain. It's so much easier to just not do it.

But I exercise everyday. I hate it but I do it. I have no choice, because my wife and kids demand it of me. My wife is 20 years younger than I, and before she'd agree to marry me, she made me promise to live to the ripe old age of 112. I'm 64 years old now, so I'm on the downhill side. Only 48 more years, and then I can rest with my fathers.

Every day I try to run. It's a terrible thing. My heart races, I drip sweat all over the place, my muscles ache, and when I'm all done I can hardly walk. But I do it because I love my family.

To anyone who knows my background, that may sound odd to you, that I hate exercise I mean. As a kid I played and worked all day, burning massive quantities of calories. I'd work in the garden, mow the lawn, play baseball, go running through the woods, swinging on vines and climbing trees. In high school I played football and baseball. Then in college I played soccer for four years. After that I officiated college soccer for 15 years. Prior to that I was in the Marines for 6 years.

So my entire life has been filled with physical exercise, tons of it, loads of it. But despite all that, there's still no denying the fact that I hate to work out. Its painful, and I don't like pain.

Two years ago my two boys came to me and asked if they could take a karate class. I said "Absolutely boys. That sounds like a great idea. Exercise is good for you and you need to learn how to protect yourself and your family."

But then they said, "Well, Dad, we were hoping that you'd do it with us." My first thought was, *Their mother put them up to this; it's all part of her 112-year longevity plan.* I balked at first, but they really wanted me to do it, so, in the end, I signed up for karate with them. I still remember the first class. There I was standing at position of attention in a white uniform, with a white belt, surrounded by midgets.

I've always thought of myself as a humble man, but ...

this was pushing my limits. All white belts start at the back of the class, with the black belts up front. And to add insult to injury, I was the oldest person in the room. I stretched my body in ways it hadn't been stretched since college. I kicked, I punched, I fell over, got back up again, punched and kicked again. Then afterwards I pretended not to be in pain so my kids wouldn't be embarrassed by me.

We've been doing this for over two years now, and it's not quite as painful as it used to be. But it's still from the devil. Some days I hurt so much that I just want to lay down and cry, but I remind myself that I'm a United States Marine, that I can do this, so I force myself to keep moving. It reminds me of what Gimli the dwarf said in *The Two Towers*: "Keep breathing. That's the key. Breathe."

The moral of the story?

WHEN ALL ELSE FAILS, WHEN I WANT TO STOP RUNning or kicking because my old body is about to give out on me, I force myself to remember the real reason I'm doing this. It's for my wife and kids. I owe it to them to be healthy and to keep on breathing. At least for now, they still need me, so I won't let them down. I choose to keep going.

Once you learn to quit, it becomes a habit.

— Vince Lombardi Jr.

Tough times don't last. Tough people do.

— Robert H. Schuller

Exercise is king. Nutrition is queen. Put them together and you've got a kingdom.

— Jack LaLanne.

My daughter ran cross country in high school and college. She had this t-shirt that read: "Pain is just weakness leaving the body." Some day when she's not looking, I'm going to burn that shirt.

— Skip Coryell

When all is said and done, I don't exercise because I love it. I hate it. But I force myself to endure the pain because it's good for my family. And that makes the pain endurable and worthwhile.

Someday, scientists are going to invent a pill that gets me in shape without all the pain and suffering of exercise, and, when they do, I'll be waiting in line to buy it.

A terrible thought just came to me. What if it's not covered by Medicaid? Oh my, best not to think about such things. In the meantime, I'll just keep breathing. Gimli was right. That's the key.

heaven
[hev-uhn]

noun
1. the abode of God, the angels,
and the spirits of the righteous after
death; the place or state of existence
of the blessed after the mortal life:

dictionary.com

2 I saw the Holy City, the new Jerusalem, coming down out of heaven from God, prepared as a bride beautifully dressed for her husband.

Revelation 21:2 (NIV)

OH MY HEAVEN!

I GREW UP IN A SMALL-TOWN BAPTIST church with a lot of old people in it. Well, at least they seemed old back then when I was a 12-year-old boy. Nowadays, at the ripened age of 64, I like to refer to them as "experienced" citizens. But back then it was impossible for me to look at life from their point of view. I was just too brand, spankin' new.

As I recall, some of them lived up north here in Michigan for 9 months out of the year and then migrated to Florida during the winter. Everyone called them snowbirds. I never understood why anyone would want to leave town just when the sledding got good, but now that my bones chill every time the thermometer dips below fifty degrees, I'm beginning to catch on.

And there's another thing I never understood, why were they all so eager to go to heaven? What's the big deal with that? As a child, my view of heaven was a boring place with angels with harps, floating on clouds, choirs singing praises to God, lots of kneeling and praying and religious stuff like that, but ... to be completely honest with you, I just didn't see the big draw.

I was in a Sunday School class a little over 10 years ago, and one of the people piped up and said how excited they were to get to heaven. Then the teacher asked us the following question:

"When you get to heaven, what is the first question you're going to ask Jesus?"

I leaned over and whispered in my wife's ear: "My first question will be "When is opening day of deer season and what is the bag limit?"

Other people chimed in with more "spiritual" discourse like "We'll get to be with God! Finally, after waiting all these years we'll get to ask him all our questions, and we'll know everything, and there'll be no more pain, no suffering, no old age," etc., etc., so on and so forth.

When I was a child I was in no hurry to meet God. After all, from a child's perspective, someone who has their whole life ahead of them, someone who has a brand new body with no aches and pains and has yet to experience the emotional pain and suffering that life inevitably brings ... why would they be eager to leave a brand new world and go to heaven?

A few months back I bought a new truck, not just a used truck that was new to me, but a brand, new truck. I've never done that before. I love everything about this vehicle. When I press the ignition button, it starts right up. It doesn't look at me and complain; it doesn't grind and grind several times and then maybe fire up the engine, it just does what it's told when it's told to do it. Of course, I know this truck won't always be like this; it won't last forever. The miles will add up; its back will get sore; it will need a shower in the morning to wake up; I may even have to pour some caffeine down its gullet if I want it to move faster.

Do you see where I'm going with this?

The moral of the story?

WHEN I WAS A CHILD LIFE WAS SO MUCH SIMPLER. I didn't have a family to take care of, little responsibility, no aches and pains and very little worry. My biggest decision was to figure out what toy to play with next. Thank God we all have a childhood.

My grandmother, was one of the greatest influences of my youth. She taught me to cook from scratch; she led me to Jesus; she told me about the depression, growing up in the muck fields, and the Second World War. She died at the ripe age of 88 years old. I remember the aches in her body, how slowly she walked and the bowing of her back. As a young man, I felt sorry for her.

I remember her funeral service to this day. People from all over the county came to say good bye to her and celebrate her life. I listened to strangers tell stories of how she'd made their lives better. I learned things about her that day, new things that made me love her even more.

4 'He will wipe every tear from their eyes.
There will be no more death or mourning or
crying or pain, for the old order of things
has passed away."

Revelation 21:4 (NIV)

"Heaven will be a place in which its in-
habitants will be freed from the fears and
insecurities that plague and haunt us in the
present life. No energy crisis there ... Free
from the economic and financial pressures
that burden us down here. Free from the fear
of personal and physical harm ... No fear
of personal failure ... Our relationship with
Him will be intimate and direct. I'm look-
ing forward to that glorious day of going to
heaven.

– Billy Graham

When all is said and done, old age is going to come. Death will come. Death can be tragic, or it can be a joyous celebration. I'm not ready for death. I guess I don't have enough aches and pains yet, but, when it does come, I want it to be a happy time; with people telling stories of how I helped make their lives better. I want kids to be running around the church getting in trouble; I want my own kids and grand kids to tell stories to each other about how I did stupid things, about how I made them laugh, about how I loved them and set them on the right path in life.

I don't know exactly what heaven is going to be like, and I probably don't need to know. When it's my time, then I'll find out. All I know is that my left lumbar is all swollen up, and that God has promised me a new body when I get to heaven. And for right now ... that's good enough for me.

tare
[tair]

noun
1. any of various vetches, especially
Vicia sativa.
2. the seed of a vetch.
3. Bible. a noxious weed, probably
the darnel.

*24 Another parable put he forth unto them,
saying, The kingdom of heaven is likened
unto a man which sowed good seed in his
field: 25 But while men slept, his enemy
came and sowed tares among the wheat, and
went his way.*

Matthew 13:24-25 (KJV)

PICK-UP TRUCK TARES

THE STRANGEST THING HAP-
pened this year. A plant started growing in the
back of my pick-up truck. A few months ago
when it started growing, my first thought was, *I need to
pull that thing before it gets too big.* But something stopped
me, and I didn't understand it at first. More on that later.

My second thought was, *Why in the world is a weed
growing in my pick-up bed, and how does that even happen?*

In the Bible, unwanted plants are called tares, and they
are symbols of things we don't want in our life. In Jesus'
parable of the wheat and the tares, I think the wheat sym-
bolizes humanity before the fall. But then Lucifer snuck
into the garden and planted a tare in order to destroy as
many humans as possible. He wanted to ruin God's beautiful garden.

Isn't it funny how weeds will grow just about any place,
but good plants, that taste good, that are useful and desir-
able, need to be nurtured and cared for? Take the tomato
plants in my garden for instance. I have to loosen the soil
around the base, I have to water them regularly; I have to
put mulch and fertilizer on as well. I also have to protect

against bugs, worms and animals that would come in and eat my plants and the final crop.

In short, it's a lot of work to produce good fruits and vegetables from seeds to final product. This spring I planted beans and a vole ate up all the seeds. My kale was growing great, but then a groundhog got inside the garden and ate them down to little nubs.

Our lives are like that too. God wants us to produce beautiful, useful fruit that benefits His kingdom and all humanity, but it's hard work and we can never let down our guard. If we do, before we know it, Satan is in the garden eating the leaves or planting weeds that choke out the good plants.

Satan is a usurper of all things left unattended.

In that regard, Satan will insert himself into our lives, slowly at first, so that you hardly notice. First one leaf starts to wilt, and then another and another. And before we know it, the whole plant is infected with disease or ravaged by rodents or choked out by tares.

Good plants must be grown in clean soil, healthy soil, free from contaminants. Our lives are no different. If you want healthy fruit in your life, then you must work hard to produce good fruit. Tend to the garden of your soul every single day.

We even have to be careful about what we let into our eyes and our minds. Listen to your self-talk. What are you telling yourself in the privacy of your own mind, the part of you that no one else knows about? Is it healthy and would God approve?

Most sin starts in the mind and takes root in the soul. Most sins can limit the final crop yield. That is, they can reduce the good you do in your life for God and those around you. Sin is a disease, planted in the garden of your life that, if nurtured, will destroy you.

And now, back to my pick-up truck.

The moral of the story?

THAT WEED IS OVER 3 FEET TALL NOW. IT RISES UP above the sides of the truck bed and it waves in the breeze when I drive. I had several people comment on it the other day. They thought it was a marijuana plant. That surprised me, because I have no idea how marijuana seeds could get into the back of my pick-up bed.

I was concerned about that, so I asked a farmer friend of mine what kind of plant it was. To my relief, he told me it was ragweed. It was growing on a bit of dirt in the corner and some rotten wood chips.

Sin will grow anywhere; it doesn't need much: minimal water, poor soil, you don't even have to "weed" it. Because, well, it's already a weed. The only thing sin needs to flourish and grow, is a willing heart. That reminds me a famous quote:

> *" 'The only thing necessary for the triumph of evil is for good men to do nothing."*

> *– Sir Edmond Burke*

If you want to seek God's face and produce good fruit, then don't just sit there … do something!

10 The thief comes only to steal and kill and destroy; I have come that they may have life, and have it to the full.

John 10:10 (NIV)

"Agriculture is the most healthful, most useful and most noble employment of man."

– George Washington

The field is the world; the good seed are the children of the kingdom; but the tares are the children of the wicked one;

Matthew 13:38 (KJV)

When all is said and done, doing nothing is the sin of slothfulness, and it will inevitably lead to a life lived short of its potential and God's will. God wants us all to live our life to its fullest, to accomplish all we can for His kingdom.

A lazy gardener will seldom produce a good, healthy crop, one free of disease and with a high yield. As Christians, we must always be vigilant. Protect your soul from tares, because once they take root, they take a toll on you and the ones you love.

Living your life to the fullest is a lot of hard work, but the joy you feel at harvest time is worth it.

chicken
[chik-uhn]

noun
1. a domestic fowl, Gallus domesti-
cus, descended from various jungle
fowl, especially the red jungle fowl,
and developed in a number of
breeds for its flesh, eggs, and feath-
ers.

dictionary.com

"Jerusalem, Jerusalem, you who kill the prophets and stone those sent to you, how often I have longed to gather your children together, as a hen gathers her chicks under her wings, and you were not willing.

Matthew 23:37 (NIV)

CHICKEN BRAINS

I'VE LONG THOUGHT THAT CHICKENS get a bad wrap. Because of their small brains and their simplistic behavior, we tend to underestimate these fowl creatures. Did you know that a chicken's brain varies in size between a lima bean and a peanut? Personally, I think that some day a chicken could be elected as president of the United States. After all, there are some similarities. That would be a fowl day indeed, but at least the chicken would do less damage. But let's keep politics out of this.

One of my favorite movies is *Fried Green Tomatoes*. In the movie, Sipsey (played by Cicely Tyson) is talking about the local sheriff who is racist.

Sipsey: Oh it don't make no kind of sense. Big ol' ox like Grady won't sit next to a colored child. But he eats eggs- shoot right outta chicken's a$$!

My three youngest kids still live at home and they run an egg business. We have about 30 hens and two somewhat useless roosters, and we average about 12 eggs a day.

I like watching the chickens strut around the yard,

scratching, digging for worms, grubs, bugs, you name it. A chicken will seldom die of starvation, simply because they'll eat almost anything. But I've noticed that chickens aren't that smart. It's frustrating for me to watch them as I throw out scratch feed for them to eat. I'll throw out a handful of food pellets and all 30 will race to gobble them up before the others get there. Then I'll throw out another handful of food, and all 30 will leave the food they are eating and race toward the new food.

What I've concluded is that either chickens are incredibly stupid, or the chicken feed is always greener on the other side of the hill. Nonetheless, I have to respect chickens, if for no other reason, than they can do something I'll never be able to achieve.

A chicken can lay an egg. While I have a much larger brain ... I can reason things out, make tools for myself, do math equations and even type on a computer, things that a chicken will never accomplish, I still have to respect them, simply because, no matter how hard I might try, I'll never be able to shoot an egg out of the my butt. I challenge you to try it some time, but I doubt you'll have any more success than I did.

All creatures, great and small, were made special by God. They have special skills, a special purpose and a reason for existence. And chickens are no different.

Think about is this way. A chicken brain is the size of a lima bean, and our brains are hundreds of times larger. You would think that we'd be smarter than them, but I look at my own life, some of the stupid things I've done over the decades, and I can't help but wonder ... am I really all that smarter than a chicken? Sometimes I screw up my relationships so bad they can't be fixed. I know better, but I still do stupid things. I have 30 chickens, but none of them have gone through a divorce. They don't go into too much debt, never been bankrupted and never lost their chicken coop in a foreclosure. When you're honest about it, us humans can do some pretty stupid things despite the size of our brain.

The moral of the story?

LOOK AT SOME MEN. THEY HAVE WONDERFUL WIVES, smart, congenial, loyal and beautiful, but then these same men, who are supposed to be smarter than a barnyard rooster, jump from one hen to the next with no regard for their wives.

That's stupid. And here's the kicker: One could forgive that stupidity, if there was some incredible redeeming quality, such as being able to shoot an egg out your backside, but men can't even do that. Every time Satan throws out a handful of feed, stupid men leave the good corn and race after the moldy feed. Not smart.

Before I go, let's clear up the age-old question: What came first, the chicken or the egg? Read the verse below and you'll know the answer.

21 So God created the great creatures of the sea and every living thing with which the water teems and that moves about in it, according to their kinds, and every winged bird according to its kind. And God saw that it was good.

Genesis 1:21 (NIV)

26 Look at the birds of the air; they do not sow or reap or store away in barns, and yet your heavenly Father feeds them. Are you not much more valuable than they?

Matthew 6:26 (NIV)

Chicken Wisdom

Nest egg – to save up a little money every week.

Scratch out a living – to earn just enough money to get by.

Don't count your chickens before they hatch – don't plan on something before it actually happens.

Don't put all your eggs in one basket – don't plan on an outcome before it actually happens.

Feather your nest – to save for the future.

When all is said and done, chickens can do some pretty amazing things. Humans can do amazing things too, but only when we follow after God, obeying His commands, worshiping Him and serving Him.

In short, chickens do great things because they act in accordance with what God created them to do. Many times us humans fight against God's will, kick against the goads, and, in the process, we ruin our lives.

Surrender to God. Don't chase the bad feed. The grass is always greener on the hill where God's will resides.

stoic
[stoh-ik]

adjective
1. of or relating to the school of philosophy founded by Zeno, who taught that people should be free from passion, unmoved by joy or grief, and submit without complaint to unavoidable necessity.

ascetic
[uh-set-ik]

noun
2. a person who leads an austerely simple life, especially one who abstains from the normal pleasures of life or denies himself or herself material satisfaction.

*4 John's clothes were made of camel's hair,
and he had a leather belt around his waist.
His food was locusts and wild honey.*

Matthew 3:4 (NIV)

JOHN (RAMBO) THE BAPTIST

WAS JOHN THE BAPTIST A stoic or an ascetic? Or, was he both? Let's think about that for a while. He certainly led an austere and simple life, one void of normal pleasures and material satisfaction. After all, the Bible says he ate locusts and wild honey. I could probably eat a locust, a small one, but I would need the honey to wash it down just to keep from throwing it back up.

When I was a younger man, I viewed myself as more of a loner. I liked the company of others, so long as I didn't have to say anything. I think that scared some people, not knowing what was going on inside my head, especially given the fact that I was sad for the most part. Many people feel uncomfortable around a quiet man with a frown. It took me several decades to figure that one out.

Perhaps that's why I was drawn to the Marine Corps. I served from 1975 to 1981. I seemed to fit right in. Shut up, do as you're told, stand up straight at position of attention.

It gave me a lot of time to think, to reflect, to figure out what made the universe tick, and that's what I appeared to enjoy the most. It didn't matter that I was austere and without a smile. From my experience, Marines who smiled usually got themselves into trouble.

I remember one time they sent me to a jungle warfare training school down in Panama. The Green Berets taught us how to make booby traps, how to keep your feet from rotting off, and how to eat and survive in the jungle. It was just a tiny bit like that Sylvester Stallone movie *Rambo: First Blood.* Do you remember this dialogue from Colonel Trautman (played by Richard Crenna.)

> *"You don't seem to want to accept the fact you're dealing with an expert in guerrilla warfare, with a man who's the best, with guns, with knives, with his bare hands. A man who's been trained to ignore pain, ignore weather, to live off the land, to eat things that would make a billy goat puke."*

I've eaten some nasty things in my life: bugs, worms, my own cooking, but I think the worst thing I ever ate was a monkey. I don't know what kind it was, because when I saw it, it was roasting on a stick over a fire. The Green Berets told us it tasted like chicken. They were liars. I think they got a kick out of tormenting Marines, watching us put the monkey meat into our mouth and forcing ourselves not to spit it back out. It's hard to describe the taste. It was like eating an animal that puked through its skin.

There is a place in life for being stoic and for being ascetic. My time in the Marine Corps prepared me for hard times that I'd soon face through two bad marriages and two painful divorces. Sometimes you just have to stuff the monkey meat in your mouth, chew it, and then quietly ask, "Thank you, sir. May I have another?"

The moral of the story?

JOHN THE BAPTIST WAS ASCETIC AND STOIC, BUT HE was also extremely passionate for what he knew to be true. He stood up for Christ and died for his beliefs.

I think that many people are either too hard or too soft. Like Rambo, during hard times, I want to be able to look adversity in the eye and say "bring it, baby!" And, of course, you have to mean it.

But I also want the ability to soften when the occasion calls for it. Sometimes I need to cry. The ability to move back and forth between hard and easy times is a skill that life teaches us, but it takes a lot of mentors and a lot of time.

I still have the ability to ignore pain and to eat things that would make a billy goat puke; however, I prefer ibuprofen with a Mocha Frappuccino chaser.

At this, Job got up and tore his robe and shaved his head. Then he fell to the ground in worship and said:

"Naked I came from my mother's womb, and naked I will depart. The Lord gave and the Lord has taken away; may the name of the Lord be praised."

In all this, Job did not sin by charging God with wrongdoing.

Job 1:20-22 (NIV)

"And if we win, we praise Him; and if we lose we praise Him. Either way. We honor Him with our actions and our attitudes."

– Facing the Giants

When all is said and done, a Christian life is a balanced life. When we start out in life, we have no idea what the world is going to throw at us. Even now, at age 64, I don't know what's going to happen even a few minutes from now.

But here's what I do know. Jesus is here for me. He has my back. No matter how painful life gets, I'll always be able to lean on Him, the rock that never moves.

I know that a Christian life is one of balance and poise. The Christian life is a life of laughter and tears. Both have value and can make you more like Jesus Christ.

forgive
[fer-giv]

verb
1. to grant pardon for or remission of (an offense, debt, etc.); absolve.
2. to give up all claim on account of; remit (a debt, obligation, etc.).
3. to grant pardon to (a person).
4. to cease to feel resentment against:
5. to cancel an indebtedness or li-ability of:

dictionary.com

When I smiled at them, they scarcely be-
lieved it; the light of my face was precious
to them.

Job 29:4 (NIV)

A KIND WORD
AND A SMILE

CAN YOU REMEMBER ALL THE way back to 1972? I was only 14 years old back then, and one of my favorite television shows was *Kung Fu*, starring David Carradine. In the series, Kwai Chang Caine is a Shaolin Monk who killed the Chinese emperor's nephew and is forced to flee China. He came to the American wild west, and for the next three TV seasons, he is chased by bounty hunters and bad men all over the territories. The show was fascinating to me as a young teen, but now I can't stand to watch it, as it's very simplistic and predictable.

The plot line was always the same. Kwai Chang Caine, affectionately known as Grasshopper by his Shaolin master, would be ridiculed and teased by bullies. So Caine would take the abuse silently, sometimes for days on end without a break. But Caine was a pacifist, so he rarely said anything other than "I have no wish to fight you." To be honest with you, I watched the show simply because I knew that Caine would, in the end, kick the snot out of all the bad guys. I loved it and my 14-year-old psyche just feasted on the violence. I remember I used to go downstairs after the show and practice being Caine. I would kick the wall, the chairs, the freezer, anything that got in my way. On more than one occasion I got in trouble for breaking things. More than anything, when I grew up, I wanted to be a karate master.

I wanted to take martial arts, but I didn't know anything about them, other than what I'd learned from David Carradine on television. I recall a man from the neighborhood, whom I respected very much, so I went to him and asked him a very simple but sincere question. "What is the best form of self-defense?" His answer was very simple, but also very disappointing to an impressionable and stupid young boy.

His short answer was: "A kind word."

I remember thinking "That's the dumbest thing I've ever heard. That's crazy!" So I rejected his advice, and never gave it another thought until about age 34 when I was going through my first divorce. It was during that time when I was most tempted to hate another person. I'd lost my kids, my wife, my house, most of my wage, and I was living hand-to-mouth for several years after that. I wanted so much to give myself over to hate, to blame, even to revenge.

I struggled with it for a long time. Finally, I learned that you can't hurt the mother of your children without also hurting your children as well. And I loved my children immeasurably. In the end, I decided to get down on my knees and pray that God would bless my ex-wife. The prayer went like this:

> *"Dear God. Please bless the labor of her hands.*
> *Help her to succeed in all she does. Bless her*
> *spiritually, mentally, emotionally and physically.*
> *Amen."*

The moral to the story?

ANYONE WHO REFUSES TO FORGIVE, EVEN WHEN they are wronged, especially when they are wronged, in the end, they will be consumed by bitterness and internal rage. Anger turned inward turns into depression.

There is one very important life skill I've learned through a lifetime of abuse and suffering: forgiveness and a kind word.

One of the most important skills we can have as Christians is the ability to readily forgive. Without it we are always seeking vengeance on those who wrong us, and there is never a shortage of injustice and cruelty.

This skill was modeled to us on the cross when Jesus forgave the ones who killed him. And if Jesus can forgive the ones who murdered Him, how can I justify doing less when someone cuts me off in traffic.

(Revised and reprinted from *Concealed Carry for Christians*.)

Therefore, as God's chosen people, holy and dearly loved, clothe yourselves with compassion, kindness, humility, gentleness and patience.

Colossians 3:12 (NIV)

"A gentle answer turns away wrath, but a harsh word stirs up anger."

– Proverbs 15:1 (NIV)

When all is said and done, a Christian life is one of kindness and forgiveness. Kind words tend to bring out the best in people, even non-Christians. I'm not talking about your feelings; I'm talking about your choices. If someone calls you a dirty, rotten SOB, you should respond in a way that helps that person see the error of their ways, regardless of your anger and hurt feelings.

And forgiveness is a choice. The word "forgive" is a verb, an action word. It requires a soulful act on your part. It has nothing to do with the person who violated you. Your forgiveness can also help them, but, more often than not, your choice to forgive protects your soul from sin and bitterness and rage.

Think about it now. Is there anyone you've failed to forgive? Don't let your anger fester. Forgive them now and restore your relationship with Christ.

meditate
[med-i-teyt]

verb
1. to engage in thought or contemplation; reflect..

dictionary.com

speed bump
[speed buhmp]

noun
1. a rounded ridge built crosswise
into the pavement of a road or driveway to force vehicles to slow down.

dictionary.com

He says, "Be still, and know that I am God;
I will be exalted among the nations, I will be
exalted in the earth."

Psalm 46:10 (NIV)

SLOW DOWN

THE YEAR **2020** WAS BITTER-
sweet for me. It was the year of Covid. The
government locked us down, established cur-
fews, social distancing and made us wash our hands every
time we touched something.

For my own personal reasons, I never went along
with it. I think I wore a mask only once during that year.
Because of that, I stayed home much of that time. I com-
plained about it to my wife, but received little sympathy.
Sara told me:

"Listen, you're always complaining about not
having time to write. Well, now you have time.
Use it!"

I hate it when she's right. Like a wise husband, I took
my wife's advice and I wrote. In short, I made lemonade
out of lemons. It took me 17 days to write a full-length
novel. I'd never done that before. The novel was titled *The
Covid Chronicles: Surviving the Upgrade.* The novel was
immediately banned from Amazon, but that's another story. We were still locked down, so I began writing another
book. (*The Covid Chronicles: Surviving the Apocalypse*)

which took me 25 days to complete. It too was banned on Amazon. Not to be intimidated, I set out to write a third book (*The Covid Chronicles: Surviving the Solstice*). I took my time on this one and it took two months.

In all my life, I'd never written so much in so short a time. It seemed counter-intuitive to me. It was a lovely paradox that thoroughly intrigued me! I was surprised, but perhaps I shouldn't have been.

The modern life moves at the speed of light, at the speed of electrons racing across my laptop screen. My cell phone rings and I feel compelled to answer it. It's difficult to go five minutes without checking my text messages or my email. And don't even get me started on social networking.

But stop and think about it for a while. What does God want us to do? Does He want us moving that fast? Does He want us to produce, produce, produce!

Ask yourself this question: Why did God create humanity? Was it so you could get rich, buy that million-dollar house, a new boat, have a 4-car garage? I doubt it. After all, isn't that why He commanded us to rest one day a week?

In a world racing at the speed of light, God has commanded us to slow down, to rest, to think, to meditate, to cogitate in our hearts and minds. But here's the kicker. When we slow down, we produce more. That's what happened to me when I wrote the three Covid Chronicle novels in record time.

A wonderful thing happened to me when I slowed down? *I heard God's voice.*

The year 2020 was a giant series of speed bumps that forced me to slow down, and when an author slows down, then he gets in touch with who he really is. He contemplates the complexity of the universe. He asks the important questions in life. Why am I here? Who is God? How can I know Him?

The moral of the story?

THE FASTER WE GO THE MORE DISTANCE WE PUT BEtween us and the Creator. Don't leave God in your rearview mirror. Take a walk. Sit on your deck and watch the grass grow. Take the time to slow down and let God catch up with you.

I'm not saying you shouldn't work hard, because there's a place for that as well. We have to support our families. Certainly the Bible speaks out against slothfulness and in favor of hard work. But sometimes we get moving so fast that we forget the true purpose of life.

Think about it today. Why did God create you? And if you can't answer the question, then think about it again tomorrow.

"If we let ourselves, we shall always be waiting for some distraction or other to end before we can really get down to our work. The only people who achieve much are those who want knowledge so badly that they seek it while the conditions are still unfavorable. Favorable conditions never come."

– C. S. Lewis

"When I am constantly running there is no time for being. When there is no time for being there is no time for listening. I will never understand the silent dying of the green pie-apple tree if I do not slow down and listen to what the Spirit is telling me, telling me of the death of trees, the death of planets, of people, and what all these deaths mean in the light of love of the Creator, who brought them all into being, who brought me into being, and you."

– Madeline L'Engle – Walking on Water

When all is said and done, when your life is over and your flesh rots into the ground, it won't matter how many cars you owned, how many business deals you clinched or how much money you made. Because now you're dead and someone else gets what you worked so hard to earn.

Nothing is more important than your relationship with Jesus Christ. God created you so that you could know Him, love Him and have fellowship with Him.

Christianity is the only religion on earth that encourages a personal friendship with the creator of the universe. Seek out that friendship in all that you do. Slow down and nurture your relationship with God. Nothing is more important.

create
[kree-eyt]

verb
1. to cause to come into being, as
something unique that would not
naturally evolve or that is not made
by ordinary processes.
2. to evolve from one's own thought
or imagination, as a work of art or an
invention.

dictionary.com

hubris
[hyoo-bris]

noun
1. excessive pride or self-confi-
dence; arrogance

dictionary.com

Remember your Creator in the days of your youth, before the days of trouble come and the years approach when you will say, "I find no pleasure in them"

Ecclesiastes 12:1 (NIV)

THE LONELY WRITER

I CAN THINK OF NO LONELIER PRO-fession than the secular writer. Think about it. He has no hope, no purpose beyond what he creates, and even that purpose has a time limit. Someday, he will die, his work will go out of print, and he'll be forever lost in the vastness of history, like a tiny speck of dust, swirling forever through the cosmos.

So what hope is there? Vanity, vanity, all is vanity. Slow down a bit Skip. Aren't you getting just a tad too heavy? Perhaps. But let's think about it for a while, and maybe I can make a graceful literary recovery.

The first story I ever wrote was in the 4th grade. It was about a boy who got trapped in a hole in a rainstorm. Thankfully, it was never published. After that, I wrote a journal in the 11th grade. I remember it was a green, spiral notebook, and I carried it with me everywhere I went. I wrote several volumes of my thoughts and musings. In fact, I still have them today. They're in a box out in my garage, buried under some junk.

Then in college I wrote my first novel. It was titled *Crossroads*, and was the most worthless, cathartic tripe ever devised by any author anywhere. It too went unpublished. I graduated from college and wrote another novel titled *A Twist of Faith*. It was about a man living alone in a cabin, searching for meaning and purpose but never finding it. This one was accepted by a few literary agents and came closer to being published.

But when I look back, I thank God that is was not, that it still lies in state in a cardboard coffin somewhere in the garage. I wrote my first two novels without the benefit of Christ. They were filled with anger, confusion, and despair. Of course, as a young man, I didn't realize they were better off unpublished, but, in retrospect, God killed them mercifully. Thank you God.

Madeleine L'Engle, in her book *Walking on Water*, talks about the Christian artist as making cosmos from chaos and about becoming a co-creator with Christ. At the time, I didn't understand what she was talking about. But after 20 years of painful mistakes, I began to comprehend why my work wasn't being accepted by publishers, and certainly not by the Christian community.

I was trying to create something worthwhile without help from the creator of the universe. Imagine the hubris I felt, being a Christian artist and not turning myself over to God. I was a fool on a fool's errand.

But after two failed marriages and a multitude of pain and suffering, God reduced me to a most desperate position: that of trusting in Him and allowing Him to use my talents for His glory and purpose.

Now, I've written and published 19 books, but I have to admit, that I don't always understand why I'm writing. From a financial standpoint, I'd be better off as a greeter at Wal-Mart, standing there mechanically, repeating the same mantra over and over again: *"Welcome to Wal-mart. We love you. Welcome to Wal-mart. We love you."*

Yes, now I'm being silly. But here's my point. Until I

crucified my *self*, until I buried my ego and laid my talent on the altar of God, then I couldn't be used by Him. God doesn't often use a selfish tool.

In fact, we are best used by God when we come to the end of our *self*, and there we find God. Go figure. God's always the last place you look.

The moral of the story?

I JUST READ SEVERAL DOZEN REJECTION LETTERS from 35 years ago, and I have to tell you that it was a miracle that I kept on writing with so little encouragement. But I did keep writing. I never gave up. In the end, I came to believe with all my heart that God had made me to write, to tell stories, to become a co-creator with Him.

And what higher calling is there? To co-create with the greatest creator of all time? Forget Tom Clancy. Forget Earnest Hemingway. From now on God is my co-author and I'm listening only to Him.

"In kairos we become what we are called to be as human beings, cocreators with God, touching on the wonder of creation."

– Madeleine L'Engle, Walking on Water

kairos
[kai·ros]

noun
1. a time when conditions are right for the accomplishment of a crucial action : the opportune and decisive moment

merriam-webster.com

When all is said and done, and when all else fails, go to God. What a foolish way to live a life. But, in fact, that's exactly how I lived my life, and that's how I wrote for the first 35 years.

As a young man, I thought I'd change the world, that I'd win the Pulitzer prize, get rich and be famous. I believe there's a certain amount of hubris in every writer. I mean, look at it this way. We have the gall to think people will actually read what we write, that we have something worthwhile to say.

In reality, nothing is left to be written. There is nothing new under the sun. The best I can hope for is to touch a few lives in a positive way, giving them hope and encouragement.

But here's the thing. Even if I knew that no one would ever read what I've written ... I would still write. And that is the mark of a true writer.

fast
[fast, fahst]

verb
1. to abstain from all food.
2. to eat only sparingly or of certain kinds of food, especially as a religious observance.

epicurean
[ep-i-kyoo-ree-uhn]

adjective
1. fond of or adapted to luxury or indulgence in sensual pleasures; having luxurious tastes or habits, especially in eating and drinking.

dictionary.com

1 Then Jesus was led by the Spirit into the wilderness to be tempted by the devil. 2 After fasting forty days and forty nights, he was hungry.

Matthew 4:1-2 (NIV)

FASTING

IN AN EARLIER CHAPTER WE TALKED about slowing down. Now let's talk about fasting. Fasting isn't something that's done very much anymore. I went online to get a definition of fasting and I had trouble finding it in all my usual places. Merriam-Webster didn't have much, and in dictionary.com I had to scroll down quite a ways to find it.

So I thought about it for a while, and I wondered to myself: *why is fasting so rare these days?* My conclusion was an exercise in the obvious.

Fasting isn't very fun. Let's be honest with each other. Eating food that tastes good is great entertainment. It pleases the senses and makes my mouth and stomach feel good. If you're over 60, then you might remember this old saying from the 1960s: *If it feels good ... do it!*

What a terrible world-in-life view. The outcome of this philosophy is predictable. If every person lives life with the end goal of feeling good, then what does that mean?

Well, that could mean a million different things. What does 'feeling good' mean to someone like Jeffrey Dahmer?

Jeffrey Dahmer, was nicknamed the Milwaukee

Cannibal or the Milwaukee Monster. He was a convicted serial killer who committed the murder and dismemberment of 17 boys and men during the years 1978 to 1991. To a man like Jeffrey Dahmer, feeling good included things like murder, dismemberment and even cannibalism.

When humanity disregards divine guidance and authority, all manner of evil can take place. Personally, I hate fasting and do it but rarely. Right now I fast 16 hours a day, because I'm trying to lose some extra weight. I find it incredibly difficult to deny my mouth and the pleasure centers of my brain that I've grown accustomed to satisfying for well over half a century.

However, while I admit that fasting isn't fun, I must add that it has its benefits.

It slows me down. It's a bit of a paradox I guess, especially when you juxtapose the two words slow and fast. A fast ... slows me down. When I stop eating with wild abandon, when I deny myself life's pleasures, then my mind naturally seems to focus less on the world and more on God; less on the physical and more on the spiritual. and the majority of eternity will not be spent on this earth satisfying all our carnal desires.

Fasting helps me stop, think, listen, and see things that I'd normally miss. It also makes me feel more grateful for all that God provides for me. I no longer take food for granted once I deny myself its pleasure for a time.

Think about it this way: the most important things in creation are not physical; they are of the spirit, and we'll not discover new spiritual truths by living an epicurean lifestyle.

The moral of the story?

AFTER FASTING FORTY DAYS AND FORTY NIGHTS, Jesus was hungry. Well, no kidding. If I fasted forty days and forty nights, I wouldn't be hungry ... I'd be dead. After my daily, 16-hour fast, I'm about ready to chew off my left arm. And you have to factor in that I'm sleeping 8 of those 16 hours.

So many of the things I hate to do in life appear to be the best things for me with the most benefit. I hate to exercise, and it's good for me. I hate to diet, and it's good for me. It's one of life's cruelties I suppose.

And it makes me wonder: Why didn't God make eating Twinkies good for me? Why can't Twinkies build muscle mass and give me more stamina and endurance? Instead, all they do is give me diabetes and make me gain more fat. It's another of life's many injustices.

I have to wonder ... will there be Twinkies in heaven? Will there be mocha Frappuccino, Mountain Dew and all manner of epicurean delights? You would think that God almighty, the creator of the universe, could re-engineer sugar to be good for us.

Yes, I know. I'm being silly again. But finite minds are like that. We can't see past the next cupcake, the next Spicy Nacho Dorito or the occasional bag of Double-stuff Oreos. (Yes, I eat the entire bag.)

In my frustration, I lift my eyes to the heavens and cry out to God. "Why, Lord, why? Why is sugar bad for me?" But, of course, He doesn't answer me. He just shakes his omnipotent and patient head back and forth before smiling at my naivete. I am a silly boy ... but God loves me anyway.

"By fasting, the body learns to obey the soul; by praying the soul learns to command the body."

William Secker

"One way to begin to see how vastly indulgent we usually are is to fast. It is a long day that is not broken by the usual three meals. One finds out what an astonishing amount of time is spent in the planning, purchasing, preparing, eating, and cleaning up of meals."

– Elisabeth Elliot

" This Man (Jesus) suddenly remarks one day, 'No one need fast while I am here.' Who is this Man who remarks that His mere presence suspends all normal rules?"

– C.S. Lewis

When all is said and done, I am a spiritual wimp. I don't like fasting. I don't like letting go of the world and clinging closely to only God. I love the world too much, with its Twinkies and snack cakes, all the artificial things that aren't good for me, and that could hasten my own death.

I need to fast more, pray more, think on God, read His word. Fasting hastens spiritual growth, and reminds us what is really important in life.

exercise
[ek-ser-sahyz]

noun
1. bodily or mental exertion, especially for the sake of training or im-
provement of health:
2. something done or performed as
a means of practice or training.

dictionary.com

indomitable
[in-dom-i-tuh-buhl]

adjective
1. that cannot be subdued or overcome, as persons, will, or courage;
unconquerable:

dictionary.com

*For physical training is of some value, but
godliness has value for all things, holding
promise for both the present life and the life
to come.*

1 Timothy 4:8 (NIV)

THE 2-MILE RUN

HAVE **I** MENTIONED YET THAT **I**
don't enjoy exercise? I think I have. Which is
odd, because I used to exercise a lot. All during my childhood I was extremely active. We didn't watch
much television, computers didn't exist yet and phones
were off limits to me, so I spent most of my day either
working for my parents, going to school or playing with
neighbor kids. Then in college I played varsity soccer for
four years. After college, I officiated high school and college soccer. It wasn't unusual for me to referee over 200
games each year up until I turned 50. After that, I stopped
so I could focus on my writing and my other businesses.
That was a mistake.

But something odd happened on my way to my golden
years. My body stopped working properly. It didn't happen all at once, and I didn't even notice until I tried to do
things that I took for granted. Things like walking up a
stairs. Running after an errant child. Riding a bike. After
10 years of inactivity, working hard at a computer, building my businesses up, I'd gotten way out of shape.

So I decided to fix that. I started running, but the extra

97

pounds I'd put on were a hinderance to me. Inevitably, I'd over do it and end up getting hurt, and that set me back even further. About 5 years ago I ruptured a disc in my back, and had to have surgery to correct it. Since then, my life has never been the same.

Despite all those challenges, I still exercise almost every day. But I have to tell ya folks; it's painful drudgery at its best, and it's sheer torture at its worst. But slowly, over a period of months, I've managed to build my body back up to the point where I can run two miles without injuring myself.

It's frustrating, because even though I have the body of a 64-year-old man, the wild, young heart of a 20-year-old Marine still beats inside my chest.

Sometimes I run on the treadmill while watching a movie I really enjoy. At other times I run a two-mile course down my street. This morning I ran a mile down our gravel road and then back again. I try to have a good attitude about it. I focus on the enjoyable parts, like the sandhill cranes over head that make a very distinct call. Because I run during the day when most people are at work, I seldom have cars pass by, but, when they do, I speed up my pace so they don't know how pitiful my stamina really is. I also speed up when I pass a neighbor's house, and then again when I pull into the driveway, so my wife and kids think I'm faster than I really am.

While running, I occupy my mind by looking at the chickory plants on the side of the road with their pretty, blue flowers. And then there are the giant, white blossoms of the queen anne's lace. About a quarter mile down the road, the houses give way to a corn field on my left and an alfalfa field on my right. They both have their distinct smells. After a cutting, the drying hay is pleasant. And in August after the corn tassels out, the smell of pollen is ripe in the air, and it overwhelms me. Then I pass a farm and the cows stop grazing and watch me as I move slowly by. I tip my imaginary hat and move on down the road.

Then there is corn, soybeans, corn and more soybeans and then back again to corn. I turn around at the end of the road and do the same thing in reverse. By now I'm loosened up, and I have a healthy spring in my step. That spring lasts for another quarter mile before I have to push myself to the finish line.

The moral of the story?

Running two miles is painful for me. I don't like it. No, more than that ... I hate it. So, why do I do it? Why do I continue to defy gravity when I know that in the end gravity will win?

At the same time every day I see a woman running down a street near us. She is grossly overweight, and she also has some type of physical deformity that hinders her gait. I can tell by the look on her face that every step she takes is painful. But still, every day she's out there, even in the cold weather. This woman inspires me, encourages me, and she puts me to shame on a daily basis.

Pete Gray was a one-armed baseball player. His right arm was cut off in an accident when he was only 6 years old. He spent most of his career in the minor leagues, but he did very well there, compiling a .333 batting average. But Pete Gray didn't stop there. He played 77 games in the major leagues with the St. Louis Browns, batting .219 and hitting 5 home runs.

mlb.com

"A friend loves at all times, and a brother is born for a time of adversity."

− Proverbs 17:17 (NIV)

When all is said and done, old age is a type of adversity. It's a natural adversity to be sure, but one that must be overcome as best you can. If you live long enough, old age is a certainty, and everyone deals with it with varying levels of success.

But here's the thing ... how you handle aging has a lot to do with how long you live and with the quality of your golden years. Most people surrender to the inevitable, content to sit in front of the television while the ravages of time take their toll.

My hope is that 10 years from now I'll still be fighting the good fight, never giving up, always struggling to do the best for my Lord with what I have left.

Never give up. Never give in. Run your best race. Who knows, perhaps your indomitable spirit may inspire someone else to do the same.

reconciliation
[rek-uhn-sil-ee-ey-shuhn]

noun
1. an act of reconciling, as when former enemies agree to an amicable
truce.

regret
[ri-gret]

verb
1. to feel sorrow or remorse for (an
act, fault, disappointment, etc.):
2. to think of with a sense of loss:

*The next day Moses came upon two
Israelites who were fighting. He tried to rec-
oncile them by saying, 'Men, you are brothers; why do you want to hurt each other?'*

Acts 7:26 (NIV)

THE RECONCILIATION

MY FATHER AND I SELDOM SAW
eye to eye. We argued when I was a child,
and that didn't change after I grew up and
moved away to college and later married. There was a period in my twenties where I went several years without
even talking to him. It was a mistake, but back then I felt
justified, and it seems we both had inherited the stubborn
gene. But I loved my father, and I always wanted to recon-
cile with him. Then, one night when I was 28 years old, I
visited him.

I'll always remember that night. It was late September
in Michigan, and the harvest smells were all around my
boyhood home. The smells of dead and dying weeds, gold-
enrod and sedge grass; they permeated the night air and
helped to set the stage for the coming showdown. I still
remember the way the grasshoppers jumped up and away
from me, like two waves parting, as I walked from the car,
through the grass to the house to talk to my father.

Once inside, all the old memories flooded back in on
me. The kitchen was in disarray. The dining room table
was cluttered with stacks of books, papers, dishes, Mason

jars filled with freshly canned tomatoes. I felt as if I was still a child, but I pushed the errant feelings back and plodded onward. What I said to him went something like this.

"Dad, I just want you to know that I love you very much, but there are some things that I have to tell you that we need to talk about."

From there, I went on to tell him specific things that he had done that had hurt me deeply. I told him about his mistakes, and how they'd made me feel unloved. Halfway through my speech, my 52-year old, battle-hardened father broke down and wept uncontrollably. I remember that he was sitting down in a chair and that I was standing. He wore a white t-shirt, like he often did, and he reached his arms out to me and I went to him. I bent down and held my father as he lay his head on my shoulder and cried. His tears soaked my shirt, and I cried as well. I remember vividly the way his muscular body heaved up and down on my shoulder as he wept. It made me feel good. Because for the first time in my life, I knew that my father, with all his flaws, loved me as much as any other father ever did. I felt loved, and I felt accepted.

After the crying was over, we sat and talked for a while about repairing our relationship, and about the things that we would do together in the future as a father and son. I left that night with a light heart, full of hope, and promise. I will remember that night for the rest of my life.

The next time I saw my father, three weeks later, he was lying in a coffin, eyes closed, resting soundly. He had died alone and unexpectedly of a blood clot. That last conversation with my father was probably one of the most important conversations of my life, and his as well. It allowed him to die as a forgiven father, and it allowed me to live on, feeling loved and accepted by the most important man in my life.

The moral of the story?

I STILL VISIT MY FATHER, AND WE TALK MORE NOW than we ever did when he was alive. His grave is on a hill overlooking the tiny town where he grew up and spent his entire life.

Some would say that this is a sad story, but not for me. My father could have lived another 100 years and a more poignant or profound and loving ending could never have been written. I regret not going to my father sooner, but, in the end, I did go to him, and we were reconciled ... for eternity.

Every generation
Blames the one before
And all of their frustrations
Come beating on your door

I know that I'm a prisoner
To all my Father held so dear
I know that I'm a hostage
To all his hopes and fears
I just wish I could have told him in the living
years

The Living Years
written by Mike Rutherford & B. A. Robertson
performed by Mike and the Mechanics

"Godly sorrow brings repentance that
leads to salvation and leaves no regret, but
worldly sorrow brings death."

2 Corinthians 7:10 (NIV)

When all is said and done, the things we sometimes regret most in life, are the things we left unsaid and the things we left undone.

My father died unexpectedly at age 52. I thank God that I bared my soul to him a mere 3 weeks before his death. If I hadn't reconciled with him, I would have regretted my inaction for the rest of my life.

Is there someone in your life that you should talk to? If so, then do it now, and avoid a lifetime of regret and sorrow.

"Why, you do not even know what will happen tomorrow. What is your life? You are a mist that appears for a little while and then vanishes."

James 4:14 (NIV)

resilience
[ri-zil-yuhns]

noun
2. the ability of a person to adjust
to or recover readily from illness,
adversity, major life changes, etc.;
buoyancy.

persevere
[pur-suh-veer]

verb
1. to persist in anything undertaken;
maintain a purpose in spite of diffi-
culty, obstacles, or discouragement;
continue steadfastly.

*As you know, we count as blessed those who
have persevered. You have heard of Job's
perseverance and have seen what the Lord
finally brought about. The Lord is full of
compassion and mercy.*

James 5:11 (NIV)

A FEW GOOD MEN

THERE ARE TWO KINDS OF PEOple in this world: those who pass Algebra class, and those who flunk. I flunked Algebra three times. And I've sometimes wondered, "Was I incredibly stupid or was I wonderfully resilient?" In retrospect, I think I was a little of both. And I suspect that people who have the internal strength (i.e., stubbornness) to take Algebra three times are also the ones who do well in Marine Corps boot camp.

So, on July 24th, 1975, just a few months after graduating from high school, I raised my right hand and swore an oath to protect the United States against all enemies foreign and domestic. A few months later I left for Marine Corps boot camp in San Diego, California.

After getting off the plane, we were loaded onto buses. It was about midnight and I still remember seeing my first palm tree, outlined in the dimness of a street light. I was fascinated with California, and so far, I was having a pretty good time. But then the bus pulled into the military base and all hell broke loose. We were greeted by four olive drab psychos.

"Move it! Move it! Move it!" I very abruptly met the four people who were going to dominate my life and change me forever. Sergeant O'Neil: "Get outta there you maggot!" Sergeant Mar: "Come on you little turd! Move it faster!" Gunnery Sergeant Preston: "You better be movin' there you little faggot!", and, last, but certainly not least, Platoon Commander, Staff Sergeant Tarver: He just stood there and smiled like Lex Luthor holding a bag of Kryptonite. I had taken my first step into a larger world.

I recall being surprised at how difficult boot camp was. We were always marching, running, doing push-ups, bends and thrusts or just being yelled at and insulted. I'd always thought I was pretty tough, and that I could handle anything, but ... after just a few hours, I was beginning to doubt myself.

I remember the daily runs along the beach. My platoon started out with 88 people, but only half of us lasted to the end of boot camp. A Navy ambulance always followed us on our exercise runs, and it didn't take long to figure out why. After a few miles men would begin to collapse on the sand. The drill instructors would gather around him and scream and yell at him to get up and running again. If he couldn't get up, then they'd leave him laying there in the sand. The ambulance would drive up to the body, load it onto a stretcher and place it in the back, then drive unceremoniously away.

And I always wondered ... what are they doing with these people? Are they killing them? And then I recalled a dystopian movie I'd watched with Charlton Heston titled *Soylent Green* where a big corporation was harvesting the population and using them for food. (Did I mention that the food tasted funny in boot camp?) Everything was green in the Marine Corps, the clothing, the vehicles, the walls, even the food. But it was a special kind of green called olive drab.

The moral of the story?

DURING MY 13 WEEKS IN BOOT CAMP, EVERY OTHER night or so I pulled guard duty, and I loved it. I suppose that sounds odd, but there has always been something about the still of the night that has drawn me to it. I love to be awake while others are asleep. I feel closer to God when that happens. There are no distractions, no conflict, no confrontation, nothing but stillness, silence and the dead of night. And it was there, walking up and down the aisles of the squad bay, where I made a deal with God. "God, you help me get through this thing, and I'll serve you the rest of my days." It was very simple, nothing profound or complex. I had just come to the end of myself, and, as luck would have it, there I found God. He'd been waiting there all along. Who would have thought that God had been waiting for me in Marine Corps boot camp? It's always the last place you look.

Semper Fidelis – Always Faithful

4 Yea, though I walk through the valley of the shadow of death, I will fear no evil: for thou art with me; thy rod and thy staff they comfort me.

Psalm 23:4 (KJV)

"They're on our left, they're on our right. They're in front of us. They're behind us. They can't get away now!"

— Colonel Chesty Puller, USMC

When all is said and done, people come to God in different ways. I was tough and stubborn, so it took Marine Corps boot camp to convince me that I needed a higher power to make it through life.

I always carried a pocket-sized new testament throughout boot camp. (Yes it was green.) And every chance I got, I opened that Bible and read. My favorite verse during that time period was this:

"God is our refuge and strength, an ever-present help in trouble."

Psalm 46:1 (NIV)

But to me, God wasn't just strength that I needed to get through a tough time. I wasn't just tapping into some convenient power source. I pledged my life to Him, and I very much wanted that personal friendship with the God of the universe.

What God did for me in boot camp, He wants to do for you as well.

reject
[ri-jekt]

verb
1. to refuse to have, take, recognize,
2. to refuse to grant (a request, demand, etc.).
3. to refuse to accept (someone or
something); rebuff:
4. to discard as useless or unsatisfac-
tory:
5. to cast out or eject; vomit.

reject
[ree-jekt]

noun
8. something rejected, as an imper-
fect article.

And the Lord told him: "Listen to all that
the people are saying to you; it is not you
they have rejected, but they have rejected me
as their king.

1 Samuel 8:7 (NIV)

REJECTION

AUTHORS LEARN TO DEAL WITH
rejection. Either that, or they end up lying on
the ash heap of literary history, alone, unsat-
isfied and unsung. And I am no stranger to rejection. The
other day I was looking for something to write about when
I ran across two notebooks filled with rejection letters
from publishers and literary agents. I didn't count them,
but there were at least 50, and those are only the ones I
kept. I know there have been hundreds of rejection letters.
from people who didn't accept my work for publication.

Even though all of the letters were decades old, it still
depressed me. Then I ran across some very special letters
from famous authors. The first one was from Madeleine
L'Engle, author of *A Wrinkle in Time*, which was later
made into a Hollywood movie. She was 68 years old at the
time she wrote.

> "No, Skip, rejection slips never stop hurting and
> there is no way we can stop taking them person-
> ally. Check out that part of "A Circle of Quiet" in
> which I tell of my 10 years of rejections."

Just a few weeks prior to that I'd received a letter from

New York Times best-selling fantasy writer Stephen R. Donaldson, author of *The Chronicles of Thomas Covenant, the Unbeliever,* which sold over 10 million copies. In his letter, he gave me some very good advice.

> "Being a writer can be extremely hard and lonely. I needed more than thirteen years of work and more than fifty rejections to achieve my first publication."

Any type of artist opens himself up to rejection and ridicule. It goes with the territory. But the rejection always hurts, even though it's not meant to be personal. To write from your heart is to open yourself up, to be vulnerable, to say to the world: "Here I am; this is what I think and believe and feel. Slay me if you will."

In an earlier chapter I quoted Madeleine L'Engle as she talked about writers being co-creators with Christ. Here's something else that Madeleine believed:

> *"The artist is a servant who is willing to be a birthgiver. In a very real sense the artist (male or female) should be like Mary who, when the angel told her that she was to bear the Messiah, was obedient to the command."*

That makes sense to me. When I write a novel, I give myself over to the characters and to the story. The story is alive just as the characters are alive, even though in reality they are fictional. If I listen carefully, then the story is born healthy and vibrant; the story becomes my baby, my offspring, whom I love and revere. So when I give my baby to the world, and it is rejected, then I'm devastated.

All artists understand this and feel it to the most basic elements of their souls. When you reject my story, you've rejected everything I live and love and hold dear. You've rejected my family.

The moral of the story?

Gᴏᴅ ɪs ᴛʜᴇ ᴏʀɪɢɪɴᴀʟ ᴀʀᴛɪsᴛ. Hᴇ ᴏᴘᴇɴᴇᴅ Hɪᴍsᴇʟғ up and made Himself vulnerable to the very characters He'd created. In truth, the Christian artist is a co-creator with Christ, however, we can never rival the original artist. We are but stilted, faded copies, like the 10th-generation photocopy of the original.

No artist in history has ever been rejected more profoundly or intimately than Jesus Christ. He came into the world but the world received Him not. Christ's art was written in blood, but it was still misunderstood and rejected by most of His creation.

As you go through your day, try to remember that if you accept God as your personal savior, then He also accepts you, warts, blemishes and all. God has accepted you, and that's the best publishing contract you could ever receive.

When the world gets you down and rejection seems overwhelming, use your sense of humor. Fire right back at them. Write the world a rejection letter that they soon won't forget. (No I never sent this out; it was just for fun.)

Dear Harper-Collins,

I have reviewed your submission guidelines, financial data, and your company mission statement. However, after thoughtful consideration, I've decided to pass on submitting my work to your company.

Please do not take this rejection personal, as there are many publishers out there, and I can only sign a contract with one. I wish you the best of luck in finding other authors as incredibly talented as myself.

Regards,

Skip Coryell

When all is said and done, rejection is a part of life that all of us struggle with. We care so much what other people think of us, and we do it religiously and to a fault.

But, in the end, it doesn't matter what others think of us; it only matters what God, our creator and our father thinks of us.

So when people reject you, don't let it slow you down. Don't take it personally. Because these same people rejected their own creator as well.

"4 As you come to him, the living Stone— rejected by humans but chosen by God and precious to him—"

1 Peter 2:4 (NIV)

mist
[mist]

noun
1. a cloudlike aggregation of minute globules of water suspended in the atmosphere at or near the earth's surface, reducing visibility to a lesser degree than fog.

dictionary.com

fog
[fog, fawg]

noun
1. a cloudlike mass or layer of minute water droplets or ice crystals near the surface of the earth, appreciably reducing visibility.
2. any darkened state of the atmosphere, or the diffused substance that causes it.

dictionary.com

*"Why, you do not even know what will hap-
pen tomorrow. What is your life? You are a
mist that appears for a little while and then
vanishes."*

James 4:14 (NIV)

THE MIST

I JUST DROVE MY TRUCK PAST THE
Mill Pond, and there was the most beautiful and
mysterious mist floating over the water. Of course
you can argue that it's just fog; that it's no big deal, but
... where's the fun in that? I happen to believe that there
is meaning and purpose in everything around us, everything we see and hear, in all of creation, and that coincidence is not coincidental.

But then again, perhaps I was meant by God to see that
mist, and that it was there to inspire me to write something important that would move at least one of my read-
ers to a deeper understanding of God and contemplation
of life. Or was it just fog?

Fog seems so droll to me. So drab, so dull, so ... com-
monplace. But mist ... now there is a special word, one with
context and purpose and meaning, one with texture and
feel, that ensnares the reader like the sirens of old. Think
about it. Why did Tolkein call them the Misty Mountains

of Angmar instead of the Foggy Mountains?

The answer is elementary, my dear Watson. Of course we know that all words have meaning, but ... just as important, words also have feelings. What does the word "misty" invoke in the reader when used in conjunction with the word "mountain"?

Far over the Misty Mountains cold,
To dungeons deep and caverns old,
We must away, ere break of day,
To seek our pale enchanted gold

— JRR Tolkein

The word "misty" is very close to the word "mystery;" they sound very much alike, but when the two words are used together, as a team, they create an ominous feel. And then when you add the alliterative quality of "Misty Mountain" well, then it's no contest. Misty Mountain leaves Foggy Mountain in the dust every time.

Words have feelings. Words have meaning. Words have rhythm. They give us information. They paint pictures. They stir emotions within us.

Take for example, the words "Give me liberty or give me death;" they stirred a nation to rise up, to fight and to give their own lives for the cause of freedom. But what if Patrick Henry had worded it differently?

"Hey, man. Give me freedom or just kill me."

There's nothing special there, nothing that moves people to action, nothing that would inspire men to rise up against the most powerful military on the planet and fight through hardship and pain and toil on to the end.

Let's take something more contemporary from the movie *Braveheart* where Mel Gibson played William Wallace.

"They may take our lives, but they'll never take ... our freedom!"

122

The moral of the story?

THE RIGHT WORDS, AT THE RIGHT TIME, SPOKEN IN the right combination, with the proper inflection, inside a powerful context can cause a nation to rise up against tyranny, even if it means they'll surely die.

So, when I drive my truck past the Mill Pond, and I see the mist rising majestically, hovering over the waters, against the backdrop of a rising sun, in brilliance, brightness and golden hue, then I see no coincidence. I see purpose. I see the power of God.

Or, then again ... maybe it's just a "cloudlike aggregation of minute globules of water suspended in the atmosphere."

You can have your fog. I choose mist.

"I like good strong words that mean something."

—Louisa May Alcott
(from "Little Women")

"To me, the greatest pleasure of writing is not what it's about, but the music the words make."

—Truman Capote

"One of the hardest things in life is having words in your heart that you can't utter."

—James Earl Jones

"Words—so innocent and powerless as they are, as standing in a dictionary, how potent for good and evil they become, in the hands of one who knows how to combine them!"

—Nathaniel Hawthorne

When all is said and done, words are what separate us from the beasts. Words are how we plan, how we think, how we feel and one way we fall down and worship our God.

Perhaps the greatest duty that the Christian writer faces, is to combine words in such a way which inspires people to do good, to serve God, to serve their fellow man, and to love all created things.

As you go through your day, measure your words wisely. Mete them out in a way that makes the world a better place to live.

practice
[prak-tis]

noun
1. habitual or customary perfor-
mance; operation:

dictionary.com

wisdom
[wiz-duhm]

noun
1. the quality or state of being wise;
knowledge of what is true or right
coupled with just judgment as to
action; sagacity, discernment, or
insight.

dictionary.com

"23 Whatever you do, work at it with all your heart, as working for the Lord, not for human masters, 24 since you know that you will receive an inheritance from the Lord as a reward. It is the Lord Christ you are serving."

Colossions 3:23 (NIV)

PRACTICE

WAS JUST SITTING AT MY DESK, looking out the window, when a white chicken, one of about 30 my kids own, jumped up into the raised vegetable garden and started eating my kale. I'm very protective about my kale. I got mad and opened the window and started yelling at the chicken. "Go on! Get out of here!" She ignored me. So I raised my voice even louder. "Go on, chicken. Get out of my kale!" She turned her little chicken head and looked at me inquisitively. I yelled a few more times, but she just put her head back down and continued eating my kale. Finally, I saw the folly in my approach and realized that the only way to save my kale was to get up off my lazy butt and chase away the chicken. Either that or put up a fence, and that's a lot more work.

So I got out of my chair, picked up a flyswatter and chased the chicken off the kale.

I write most of my best stories in my driveway, either in the cab of my truck or the office I've set up in my fifth wheel camper. I try to write everyday, but can't always, because sometimes I actually have to make a living.

Many of my friends are in awe of my ability to write, primarily because they've never done it before, and they couldn't string ten words together to save their life. They've convinced themselves that writing is some mystical power that you either have or you don't. Personally, I think writing is a talent that most can achieve, at least tolerably well, but it takes practice.

One of my favorite movies is the BBC version of *Pride and Prejudice* with Colin Firth and Jennifer Ehle. In one scene, Elizabeth, Darcy and Colonel Fitzwilliam discuss why Darcy refuses to talk as much as others.

> *'I certainly have not the talent which some people possess,' said Darcy, 'of conversing easily with those I have never seen before.*
>
> *'My fingers,' said Elizabeth, 'do not move over this instrument in the masterly manner which I see so many women's do. ... But then I have always supposed it to be my own fault – because I would not take the trouble of practising.*
>
> *– Jane Austen. Pride and Prejudice*

Perhaps writing talent is gained in the same manner as wisdom. We achieve wisdom through study, watching other people make mistakes, and most importantly, by making mistakes of our own. I should know. I'm on my third marriage now, and I'm still practicing, trying desperately to get it right.

One of the things that many successful authors agree on is this: if you want to get good at writing, then you have to practice. And not just a casual affair, but practice and repetition in earnest, not wavering and never giving up. Like any athlete or craftsman, the skill must be honed to a razor's edge, and the only way to do that is to take the time and effort required.

Since I began this chapter, that blasted chicken has jumped into the kale garden five times, forcing me to get off my butt and chase her away. Eventually, the chicken's passion for my kale will win out, because she wants to eat my plants more than I want to save them. I have other things that are more important.

The moral of the story?

To BE SUCCESSFUL AT ANYTHING TAKES HARD WORK and perseverance over a long period of time. That quality of staying power only comes when your passion drives you to practice unceasing and to never give up. And that's why most people will never be writers ... or professional athletes, or billionaires.

In order to become an excellent writer, you have to spend a lot of time writing garbage that later on will shame you into hiding it in the garage.

"You don't write because you want to say something; you write because you have something to say."

— *F. Scott Fitzgerald*

"There is nothing to writing. All you do is sit down at the typewriter and bleed."

— *Ernest Hemingway*

"Start writing, no matter what. The water does not flow until the faucet is turned on."

— *Louis L'Amour*

"A professional writer is an amateur who didn't quit."

— *Richard Bach*

"I am not at all in a humor for writing; I must write on until I am."

— *Jane Austen*

When all is said and done, writing is not a superpower; writing is no different than any other skill set. If you work hard enough, then you'll eventually get better at it.

Certainly some people have more natural talent than others, but my experience is this: the more you write, the more natural ability you seem to find.

Here's what makes a good writer. When I wake up in the middle of the night with an idea, I can't get back to sleep until I go to the computer and write. Sometimes I lay there for hours just thinking, and trying to make the thoughts go away.

To put it in modern terms, I have to practice more than most, simply because I have less natural talent. I certainly must be the Rocky Balboa of the writing world.

self-esteem
[self-i-steem]

noun
1. a realistic respect for or favorable impression of oneself; self-respect.

curse
[kurs]

noun
1. the expression of a wish that misfortune, evil, doom, etc., befall a person, group, etc.

"Before I formed you in the womb I knew you, before you were born I set you apart; I appointed you as a prophet to the nations."

Jeremiah 1:5 (NIV)

SELF ESTEEM

THERE ARE SPECIAL TIMES IN EVery person's life that are etched in stone, carved into rock with images, words, and feelings. They serve to mold us, shape us, warp us, for better or for worse, and through no fault of our own, these special times are with us to stay, forever imbued with power and permanence as they attempt to steer us through life, either hopelessly off track, or straight ahead on that coveted True North compass heading of life. My childhood was jam-packed with moments like that.

I can still remember the most hurtful and powerful words my father ever said to me: "Son, the best part of you went running down your mother's leg!" With those words, my father prophesied and cemented my own illegitimate view of my self worthlessness. I must have been 14 years old at the time, so I refused to cry, not wanting to give him the satisfaction.

At the time, I remember feeling angry and bitter, wanting to lash out at anyone close to me, and I suppose my younger brothers and sisters felt the undeserved heat of my wrath on more than one occasion. But I think the anger of the moment was just a secondary emotion that I used to protect myself from the pain of my father's disdain and disapproval. At the time, I didn't want to give him his due, but I can no longer deny that my father was indeed the biggest influence on my young life.

I can also remember an incredible anger and fear of God. Over the years, I've come to realize that my view of God the Father was in many ways shaped by my relationship with my earthly father. I suppose it makes sense. I didn't understand that until I became a father myself. Parenthood is packed with personal epiphanies to anyone hungering for the Truth.

Over the decades I've come to realize that everything on earth is a symbol of something in the Bible, whether it be numbers or words or rocks or trees or even people. Every created thing has its own purpose and meaning.

At 14 years of age, I didn't even know what self-esteem meant. I'd never even heard the term before. I didn't learn about any of that until college. Since then I've come to realize that my father's prophesy has followed me through space and time even to the present day. Everything I do and say about my own self-worth is filtered through the tainted prism of my father, how he molded me and how he shaped me.

Even now, after writing 19 books, I still doubt myself. Every time I sit down in front of the keyboard, I tremble, wondering to myself, can I do this? Who do I think I am? What could you possibly have to say that others will want to read? It is a weakness in my personality. Or is it?

The moral of the story?

THERE ARE TWO SIDES TO EVERY COIN, AND TWO sides to every person. Deep inside me is the curse that my father pronounced on me at age 14. It is the thorn in my flesh, the doubt that I carry with me everywhere I go, no matter what I do.

It reminds me of the story of Joseph. His brothers sold him into slavery, violated him, took away his life with a father who really loved him. That was a profound loss. But I've learned that with every act of evil, there is a counter-act of goodness to balance it.

Joseph was made stronger by surviving the evil his brothers thrust upon him.

20 You intended to harm me, but God intended it
for good to accomplish what is now being done,
the saving of many lives.

Genesis 50:20 (NIV)

Every time I try to accomplish something good, I fight against the pronouncement my father gave to me. I have to hit the manual override button and force myself to remember who God, my heavenly father, says I really am.

In the end, I get my self-worth from God the Father, who looked at me and said, "he is my child, and I love him."

9 But he said to me, "My grace is sufficient for you, for my power is made perfect in weakness." Therefore I will boast all the more gladly about my weaknesses, so that Christ's power may rest on me. 10 That is why, for Christ's sake, I delight in weaknesses, in insults, in hardships, in persecutions, in difficulties. For when I am weak, then I am strong.

2 Corinthians 12:9-11 (NIV)

When all is said and done, our greatest weakness can also become our greatest strength. As a young man I was forced to look outside myself for meaning and purpose and self-esteem. That search brought me to God.

In boot camp I came to the end of myself and found God. And when I found God, I found my true self-worth. I am a child of God. He created me. And then He pronounced me as good.

God would never send His son to die for me if He thought I was a hopeless case.

The next time you doubt your self-worth, remind yourself that you are a child of the king ... and that makes you royalty.

Just like Joseph, in our weakness ... we are made strong.

comfort
[kuhm-fert]

verb
1. to soothe, console, or reassure;
bring cheer to:

dictionary.com

"Everything with a beginning has an ending."

– *Matt the Happy Prepper*
(from "The Mad American")

3 Praise be to the God and Father of our Lord Jesus Christ, the Father of compassion and the God of all comfort, 4 who comforts us in all our troubles, so that we can comfort those in any trouble with the comfort we ourselves receive from God.

2 Corinthians 1:3-4 (NIV)

HARD TIMES

'M 64 YEARS OLD, AND I'M A VERY happy man. Sara and I have been married 17 years, and we have three very happy children. But it wasn't always so, and certainly I am no stranger to hard times. I've had more than my share of adversity, pain and suffering.

I remember one night in particular. I was on my second marriage. I had two kids from the first marriage and two from the second. My second wife had a drinking and alcohol problem, and it wasn't unusual for her to meet me at the door when I got home from work, jump into the car and not return until the following morning when it was time for me to go to work again.

On one such night, I'd had enough of it and vowed to make her stop. She met me at the door, handed our baby to me and jumped in the car as quickly as she could. I stepped behind the car, blocking her way. I knew in my heart that she wouldn't run over me while I held our child.

She didn't hesitate. She started the engine, put the car in reverse and floored the accelerator. I barely got out of the way in time.

Things like this continued off and on for a period of years. I loved her and wanted our marriage to work and for us to raise a happy family together. But that was not to be.

I recall another evening I came home from working 12 hours and she was on the phone talking to someone. Our one-year-old son, Phillip, was nestled on her left hip, and the phone was cradled against her right ear. As soon as she saw me walk in, all the color drained from her face.

I knew immediately who she was talking to. I walked up to her and asked, "Is that him?"

She said, "Yes."

Surprisingly, she didn't resist when I reached over and took the phone.

I spoke to the man calmly but firmly. I explained that I was her husband, that we had two young children, and that he had no business sleeping with my wife. I told him he was breaking up our family and that he needed to stop as quickly as possible.

He didn't answer at first but I could hear him weeping on the other end of the phone. To make a long story short, he apologized to me and vowed to stop seeing my wife. I hadn't expected myself to feel sorry for the man. A month later I caught them together again.

You see, the adulterous man wasn't the main problem. Certainly he was guilty, but ... without a consenting partner, there would be no sin. Later on I learned that my second wife had many affairs, and I'll never know how many, nor is it important that I know. They are all forgiven. In fact, she went to alcoholics anonymous with the express purpose of finding new lovers and drinking partners.

The marriage limped on for a few more years, like a

cancer, going into and out of remission, but, in the end, my marriage ended.

The moral of the story?

THAT HAPPENED 25 YEARS AGO, BUT IT STILL SADdens me to remember it. Those were hard times, and they caused me many years of incredible pain. But in retrospect, they helped to make me who I am today.

Most of us wonder ... *why does a loving God allow pain?* Well, that's a complicated question with a multi-faceted answer. But here's what I do know.

All that pain caused by adultery and addiction; it could have ruined me, caused me to abandon God and never return.

Hard times like these will either make you a better person or a worse person. The most important part of pain is in how you respond and heal.

"Hard times cause pain, and pain changes people. It makes you either a better person or a worse person.

> – Matt the Happy Prepper
> (from "The Mad American")

"Hard times create strong men. Strong men create good times. Good times create weak men. And, weak men create hard times."

> – G. Michael Hopf
> (from "Those Who Remain")

"The primary job that any writer faces is to tell a story out of human experience – I mean by that, universal, mutual experience, the anguishes and troubles and griefs of the human heart, which is universal, without re-gard to race, or time or condition. He wants to tell you something which has seemed to him so true, so moving, either comic or tragic, that it's worth preserving."

> – William Faulkner

When all is said and done, pain is a part of life for everyone. Perhaps you're going through hard times right now, and you're discouraged and depressed.

The most important part of pain is in how you grow through it. You don't have to enjoy the pain; that would be crazy. But you do have to somehow end up on the other side.

If you cling to God, hold on to Him with all your might, you'll make it to a world beyond pain. But if you quit, give in to the suffering, you'll end up bitter and alone.

God doesn't always take away the pain, but He does want to hold your hand and walk beside you. Don't blame Him. He's not the problem ... He's the solution.

choice
[chois]

noun
1. an act or instance of choosing;
selection:
2. the right, power, or opportunity to
choose; option:

freewill
[free-wil]

adjective
1. made or done freely or of one's
own accord; voluntary:

I will sacrifice a freewill offering to
you; I will praise your name, Lord,
for it is good.

Psalm 54:6 (NIV)

THE RABBIT HOLE

"**T**HIS IS YOUR LAST CHANCE.** After this, there is no turning back. You take the blue pill, the story ends. You wake up in your bed and believe whatever you want to believe. You take the red pill. You stay in wonderland, and I show you how deep the rabbit hole goes."

Those were the words of Morpheus, played by Laurence Fishburne in the movie "*The Matrix.*" He was talking to Neo, played by Keanu Reeves. In his left hand, he held a shiny blue capsule, and in his right, he held the red. It was come to Jesus time for Neo. He had spent his entire life following the white rabbit, searching for that invisible unknown, that mysterious haunting, that ever-elusive unknown, nagging at his soul, hooking him, pulling him in and reeling him toward its maw.

There is a matrix in every person's life, and we all have a white rabbit to follow. We can take the red pill, and all our questions will be answered, but at what price? We can take the blue pill, and go on with our uncomplicated, unsearching, oblivious lives. Which pill did you take?

Whatever your choice, there is a price to pay. We live and die based on the decisions we make. The world is cause and effect – always has been, always will be. I suspect that most of us take the blue pill, because it seems safer, less precarious, less demanding, with few or no surprises.

But that incessant red pill; it's a muse, always calling out, always reaching out for the artist and pioneer inside us. The red pill wants us to follow, no, demands it, and some of us have the need to heed its call, the need to swallow it hook, line, and sinker.

Many years ago I had my own personal "Neo moment." But instead of Morpheus sitting across from me, it was God almighty. He held out both his hands, palms up and looked me full in the eyes. His face was shining and trusting and full of power. The left palm opened, and the blue pill lay there glistening and enticing, full of known promise.

"Take the blue pill, and continue through your life oblivious to my plan."

Then his right hand opened and I audibly caught my breath. The red pill glowed in the light, evanescent at first, but growing more and more constant the longer I looked at it, until, finally, my eyes were transfixed on the immutable light inside the pill.

"Take the red pill, and I show you how deep the rabbit hole goes."

As I pondered God's offer, the words of Morpheus came back to me, ringing out, tolling for me.

"Let me tell you why you're here. You're here because you know something. What you know you can't explain. But you feel it. You've felt it your entire life, that there's something wrong with the world. You don't know what it is, but it's there, like a splinter in your mind, driving you mad. It is this feeling that has brought you to me."

So there I was, sitting in the presence of God, knowing that I had been following his white rabbit my whole life, knowing that if I took the blue pill, I would always wonder about the rabbit hole, that incessant splinter in my mind, and curse my lack of courage. The unrealized curiosity would kill me.

The moral of the story?

So I took the red pill. I swallowed the whole bottle and never looked back. I'm so deep inside the rabbit hole now that I'll never come out. But that's okay, because I'm happy. I don't want to come out. Every new day brings more secrets to light and more treasures to find.

I overcame my fears. I acted on the strongest part of my character, and I have no regrets.

"If a thing is free to be good it is also free to be bad. And free will is what has made evil possible. Why, then, did God give them free will? Because free will, though it makes evil possible, is also the only thing that makes possible any love or goodness or joy worth having."

— C.S. Lewis

"There is no space where God is not. Yet, I can eliminate Him from the space which is me. And if He has granted me that kind of power, I should probably be far too scared to ever use it."

— Craig D. Lounsbrough

"For we do not run to Christ on our feet but by faith; not with the movement of the body, but with the freewill of the heart."

— Augustine of Hippo

When all is said and done, I think, perhaps, my greatest fear was best voiced by Henry David Thoreau who said, "Most men lead lives of quiet desperation, and go to the grave with the song still in them."

To go to one's grave having never graced the world with your song, is to go to your grave unwept, unhonored and unsung.

So I encourage you now. Take the red pill. Sing the world your song, the one that struggles to burst from your heart, the song given to you by God before the foundations of the earth, with your voice held steady and strong, with no apologies and no regrets. Sing your song, the one placed in your heart by God at birth, lest the splinter drive you mad.

hope
[hohp]

noun
1. the feeling that what is wanted
can be had or that events will turn
out for the best.

dictionary.com

despair
[dih-spair]

verb
3. to lose, give up, or be without
hope

dictionary.com

"At least there is hope for a tree: If it is cut down, it will sprout again, and its new shoots will not fail."

Job 14:7 (NIV)

THE MULBERRY TREE

THERE'S AN OLD SONG I USED TO sing when I was little. It went like this:

"Here we go round the mulberry bush, the mulberry bush, the mulberry bush. Here we go round the mulberry bush, so early in the morning."

I like the song, because it reminds me of an earlier time, a time of innocence, a time of carefree childhood when I could romp the woods and fields without the stress of adulthood.

As I write this chapter, I'm sitting behind my house, and my four-month-old son, Cedar, is in his car seat beside me. We're in the middle of the woods, and we're just sitting here. He is cooing quietly, and I'm just listening to the birds and the bugs. It is mid-July, and I can hear the Cicadas in the treetops, buzzing loudly; they only do that in the heat of the summer. My son just started crying, so I handed him a stick and he's good for another 10 minutes. I wish life could be so simple now as it was when we were kids.

It's true that much of my childhood was painful, but much of it, the part of me that grew up climbing trees, swinging on grape vines, and jumping into and over mud puddles, that part of it, gave me a lifelong appreciation and longing for all of nature, anything wild and free. On a good day, I felt like Tom Sawyer. On a bad day, I felt like Huckleberry Finn.

I recall that my cousin, Randy, and my brother, John, spent a lot of time together with me in trees. Sometimes they were mulberry trees, and we would pick the purple berries and eat them until we could hold no more. And while we picked, we talked – about frogs, Superman, and other silly things. It was my down time, my break from the stress of family jihad. I loved it up in those trees, up above, so high, looking down on the world, feeling the breeze on my cheeks, and safe from the yelling, the screaming, the fighting, and the insults. Up in the top of the mulberry tree, I was the boy king, and no one could touch me.

I recall many decades ago, while deep in the throes of agony and pain, I was nearing the end of my hope. It was the dead of winter in all its harshness. The air was cold, and the wind made it even more so. I didn't know this at the time, but most people take their own lives because they start believing that their pain is permanent. Despair is a very dangerous place to remain.

I was living in Grand Rapids at the time, so I spent much of my day surrounded by brick, steel and mortar. Not a happy place for a born-and-bred country boy.

I recall leaving an office building and walking to my car. I paused and looked around, contemplating how much longer this pain and suffering would last, as I stood on the stark pavement shivering in the cold.

The moral of the story?

IT WAS THEN I NOTICED THE SMALL TREE WITH A branch overhanging my beat-up, old car. Somehow, it looked familiar to me. I walked up to it, grasped the branch in my hand and took a closer look. It was a mulberry tree.

Just holding the branch in my hand flooded back old memories of my brother and my cousin, how we sat in the branches, ate the berries and talked about unimportant things that only a pre-teen would deem essential. I think I even smiled.

And that's when I noticed something that I'd never seen before. There was a bud attached to the twig, not one, but many. There were hundreds of buds on the tree, promises of spring, and I was reminded that everything with a beginning has an ending. My pain would not last forever. It was finite. I snapped off a twig, raised it to my nose and smelled it. Then I put it on the dash of my car and kept it there as a reminder of the spring.

"I don't think of all the misery, but of the beauty that still remains."

– Anne Frank

"May your choices reflect your hopes, not your fears."

– Nelson Mandela

"The darkest hours are just before dawn"

– Thomas Fuller

"For I know the plans I have for you," declares the Lord, "plans to prosper you and not to harm you, plans to give you hope and a future."

Jeremiah 29:11 (NIV)

When all is said and done, spring isn't just a hope ... it's a certainty. It will come because it has to come. It will come because God has foreordained it to be. Nature has no choice but to follow the rules of the one who created her.

The pain of man lasts for but a season. However, spring will always come, just as the sun will always rise.

Sometimes we get so wrapped up in our desperate circumstances that we can't see past our own pain. Maybe that's happening to you right now. If it is, take a step back and remind yourself that the love of God lasts forever.

Always remember ... the bud of the mulberry isn't just a hope ... it's a promise.

tenacity
[tuh-nas-i-tee]

noun
1. the quality of being tenacious, or
of holding fast; persistence:

resolute
[rez-uh-loot]

adjective
1. firmly resolved or determined; set
in purpose or opinion:

"As the time approached for him to be taken up to heaven, Jesus resolutely set out for Jerusalem."

Luke 9:51 (NIV)

WE HAVE TWO LIVES

WHEN THE **BLOCKBUSTER** movie *The Natural* was released on May 11th, 1984, it was widely acclaimed as one of the best baseball movies of all time and was nominated for four Oscars. However, despite the critical and public acclaim, this movie had less to do with baseball, and more to do with life. Perhaps that is why *The Natural* is a great movie. It's a story that moves us.

Sitting in a café in 1939, reminiscing about their childhood together, Roy Hobbs (played by Robert Redford) and Iris Gaines (played by Glenn Close) talk about what has happened since they were kids, and all the unexpected curves that life has thrown at them.

"What happened to you Roy?"

"My life didn't turn out the way I expected."

That was an understatement. Here he was, the great Roy Hobbs, the most talented player that baseball had ever known, and he had spent the last 16 years of his life as

157

a drifter, accomplishing nothing with his incredible God-given talents.

Have you ever felt like Roy Hobbs? I have, and on more than one occasion I have asked myself, "What happened to you Skip?" And my answer is always the same. "My life didn't turn out the way I expected." It's a universal truth, one that runs deep in the race, deep in the grain of our existence. Some of us plan; some of us don't. But, in the end, it all seems so futile. Because when our lives near their end, and we sit back in our rockers and look behind through the decades of our life, very little went according to our schedule and plan. It would seem, perhaps, that life has a mind of its own.

Later, in the hospital, after the doctor tells Roy that he can never play baseball again without risking his life, Iris visits his bedside.

"Doc says I have to quit playing baseball."

"Why?"

"Some mistakes I guess we never stop paying for."

Yes, it's true. I can look at my own life and recognize the crossroads, the missed turns, the places where I went astray. Sometimes I knew I was screwing up, while at others, I was totally blind-sided. Early on, I was just plain young and dumb.

Roy Hobbs sits up in bed talking to his old friend Iris, with only a few pillows to prop him up. He is all but beaten.

"Things sure turned out different."

"In what way?"

Roy shakes his head in confusion.

"Different. For 16 years I've lived with the idea that I could have been the best in the game."

Iris beams at him happily.

"You're so good now!"

"I could have been better. I could have broke every record in the book."

Iris seems disappointed by Roy's answer and her smile fades away before replying.

"You know I believe we have two lives."

"How . . . what do you mean?"

"The life we learn with, and the life we live with after that. With or without the records, they'll remember you. Think of all those young boys you've influenced. There's so many of them."

The moral of the story?

IT IS THE BOTTOM OF THE NINTH, TWO MEN ON BASE, two outs, and Roy Hobbs is up to bat. He is wounded, with blood seeping from his left side, while a young farm boy from Nebraska is attacking him with the fastest baseball in the league. There are two strikes against him, and Roy can barely stand.

Tension is in the air as lightning strikes off in the distance. Roy settles in, the wind-up, the pitch. Roy swings one final time and the ball sails out of the park!

"Many of life's failures are people who did not realize how close they were to success when they gave up."

— *Thomas A. Edison*

"Fish," he said softly, aloud, "I'll stay with you until I am dead."

— *Ernest Hemingway*
(The Old Man and the Sea)

"Often it is tenacity, not talent, that rules the day."

— *Julia Cameron*
(Finding Water: The Art of Perseverance)

"My motto was always to keep swinging. Whether I was in a slump or feeling badly or having trouble off the field, the only thing to do was keep swinging."

— *Hank Aaron*

When all is said and done, Roy Hobbs is right. Some mistakes stay with us the rest of our lives, but that's okay. We all make mistakes. The bigger question is what are you going to do with those mistakes? Are you going to walk back to the dugout defeated, or are you going to hunker down and take the pitch that life has to give you.

Take it from a man who has swung and missed. If you're going to go down, then go down swinging. Never give up. Life is like baseball, but you're not limited to only three strikes. You can stand up there and swing as many times as you want.

God has a plan for your life, but when you screw that one up, don't worry, He has a plan B ... and a plan C ... and a plan ... well, you get the idea. God is tenacious and He'll never give up on you; so don't you give up on Him!

indefatigable
[in-di-fat-i-guh-buhl]

adjective
1. incapable of being tired out; not
yielding to fatigue; untiring.

overcome
[oh-ver-kuhm]

verb
1. to get the better of in a struggle or
conflict; conquer; defeat:

*"7 For the Spirit God gave us does not
make us timid, but gives us power, love and
self-discipline."*

2 Timothy 1:7 (NIV)

DOING PULL-UPS

BACK IN **1976,** IF YOU MADE IT
straight through boot camp without any injuries or other set-backs, then you could get
through it in 11 weeks. But Private Strang was an unusual
man. When I met him, he'd been in Marine Corps boot
camp for about nine months. To say the least, that's not
normal. It's different now, but back then, you could, in
theory, spend years in boot camp provided you never did
one thing ... give up.

You see, Private Strang was tall and skinny with a naturally weak upper body. At best, if he tried really hard, and
the wind was blowing in the right direction, all the planets
were lined up perfectly, and he prayed hard to almighty
God, then Private Strang, on a good day, could do two
pull ups. Unfortunately, the requirement for graduating
Marine Corps boot camp was three.

Most of us recruits were fascinated by Private Strang

simply because he'd endured boot camp for such a long time. There was something special about him. He could have given up and gone back home to momma and poppa, but he didn't. He hung in there, refusing to fail, refusing to pack it in and admit defeat. Even though the rest of us could run faster, shoot better and out-march Private Strang, he nonetheless commanded our undying respect and devotion.

Our four drill instructors had faith in him as well and were determined that he would graduate with our platoon. All of us helped him, cheered him on, and worked with him every minute of each day to make him better, so that he could, at the moment of truth, do those three elusive pull-ups when he took his final Physical Fitness Test before graduation.

I wish I knew Private Strang's first name, but I just don't. No one in boot camp ever knew anyone's first name. It was against the rules. Our names were stamped in black ink with military block letters on every article of clothing we were issued. My new name in boot camp was "Private Coryell." People with common last names were denoted by adding their initials at the end, such as, Rivera MA or Smith DM.

Private Strang was a good Marine recruit. He always gave his best, always had a superior attitude, and he never gave up. In the final analysis, when Private Strang was weighed and measured, he managed to pass his Physical Fitness Test. He did his three pull-ups.

Now, I know that sounds a bit silly to some of you. You might be thinking ... *how can a Marine be so weak in his upper body? Even I can do three pull-ups!* But you ask that question only because you don't understand the most important quality of being a United States Marine. The most important measure of a Marine isn't in how many pull-ups he can do or weight he can lift or the size of his biceps. A Marine is measured by the size of his heart and the strength of his spirit.

The moral of the story?

WHEN THE MARINE CORPS FIGHTS, WE HAVE BUT one rule. Never give up ... leave it all on the battle field. If you die ... you die. But you never surrender.

As a Christian soldier, the rules are the same. You never give up the fight. No matter what life throws at you, you never give in to despair; you never slow down or stay discouraged. You keep on going even when life gets so hard that you feel like dying.

When I was in boot camp, I came to the end of myself, to the end of my own strength, and that's when I found the strength of God. I called on Him to help me and He did. As you go through your day, remind yourself that you are a warrior of God. When adversity attacks, then fight back. Every attempt to defeat you should strengthen your resolve.

"We shall go on to the end, we shall fight in France, we shall fight on the seas and oceans, we shall fight with growing confidence and growing strength in the air, we shall defend our island, whatever the cost may be. We shall fight on the beaches, we shall fight on the landing grounds, we shall fight in the fields and in the streets, we shall fight in the hills; we shall never surrender..."

– Winston Churchill

"Only those who will risk going too far can possibly find out how far one can go."

– T.S. Elliot

"No one will hit you harder than life itself. It doesn't matter how hard you hit back. It's about how much you can take, and keep fighting, how much you can suffer and keep moving forward. That's how you win."

– Sylvester Stallone

When all is said and done, we are all warriors in God's army. We volunteered to fight against evil. We swore an oath to fight to the end in support of our Lord and Savior Jesus Christ.

No matter what evil may assail us ... we will never give up. No matter how many battles we lose ... we will never give in. To a Christian, there is no surrender ... only advance.

accountable
[uh-koun-tuh-buhl]

adjective
1. subject to the obligation to report,
explain, or justify something; respon-
sible; answerable.

dictionary.com

*"But Joshua spared Rahab the prostitute,
with her family and all who belonged to her,
because she hid the men Joshua had sent as
spies to Jericho—and she lives among the
Israelites to this day."*

Joshua 46:25 (NIV)

ACCOUNTABILITY

AFTER GRADUATION FROM BOOT camp, I was given 2 days leave before I had to report in at Camp Pendleton. I didn't know what else to do, so I walked to downtown San Diego with a buddy of mine. Terry was my childhood friend and we had enlisted on the buddy program. He was from a different background than I: more experienced, and at the young age of 18, already a man of the world so to speak, at least by my rural, naïve standards.

So when we walked down the seedy avenue in San Diego, being propositioned every ten feet by a young woman or a drug dealer, Terry seemed to take it all in stride. I, on the other hand, had my eyes so wide open they nearly fell out of their sockets.

Finally, we arrived at our hotel room unmolested. I had never been to a hotel, and I was looking forward to relaxing on the bed and watching a television with over ten channels!

Three fellow Marines met us and told us not to enter our room. I asked why not.

Our buddy was smiling from ear to ear, and his voice barely contained his excitement.

"Rivera's in there with a girl. She's doing all of us!"

Just then the connecting suite door opened up and a very happy Rivera walked out. The woman opened the door partway and stuck her head out. I remember my first thought: this woman is very attractive. I was surprised that she was no older than the rest of us, a mere kid starting out in life just like me. She had dark eyes, and light brown skin with a slight Hispanic accent.

"Okay, which one of you is next?"

The Marine who had opened the door for us rushed right in and the suite door closed behind him and locked. I remember asking "How long are they going to be in my room?" No one answered me, and then a more terrifying thought occurred to me: "Hey! Whose bed are they using?" No one seemed to know.

A few minutes later, the door opened again and out marched the world's happiest Marine. The girl stuck her head out again and smiled warmly. "Okay, who's next?" I remember she had a blanket wrapped around her naked body. I struggled to turn away, but I couldn't. I noticed that she was slightly pudgy, but not so overweight as to render herself unattractive. No one said anything, and then she looked at me and smiled. Her eyes were dark and beautiful, and her long, black hair cascaded down around her bare shoulders. There was a moment of silence that seemed like forever. Then my buddies goaded me. "Go on Coryell! Get in there! Do it!"

Have you ever had a million different thoughts running through your head at the same time? Have you ever felt a myriad of emotions, all conflicting, all seemingly diametrically opposed? That's how it was.

It's odd the things we remember after so many years have passed. But what I remember most is wanting to know her name, wanting to sit and talk, to feel emotionally connected to her, to know that she cared about me. But the cold truth was – I didn't even know her name. None of us did. I have long wondered about that.

I looked down at the light green floor tiles and finally answered. "No thank you."

She left, and my first night in a hotel, I slept on the floor.

The moral of the story?

IN RETROSPECT, I'VE TRIED MANY TIMES TO DECIPHER why I turned that girl away. Yes, I understand she was just a prostitute, but I can't help but feel a confusing mix of emotions toward her. I wanted her ... but I didn't want to want her.

I have long contended that the weakest part of a man is just below the waist, and I'm a man and therefore no exception to this human law. However, on this one lonely night in a San Diego hotel room, the weakest part of my character was overcome by something stronger. But to this day, 40 years later, I can't tell you for sure what it was. Was it fear? Was it self-righteousness? Was it my promise to God?

One thing is for certain: it wasn't the twenty dollars.

"By faith the prostitute Rahab, because she welcomed the spies, was not killed with those who were disobedient."

Hebrews 11:31 (NIV)

"Do you not know that he who unites himself with a prostitute is one with her in body? For it is said, 'The two will become one flesh.'"

1 Corinthians 6:16 (NIV)

"Flee from sexual immorality. All other sins a person commits are outside the body, but whoever sins sexually, sins against their own body."

1 Corinthians 6:18 (NIV)

"Flee the evil desires of youth and pursue righteousness, faith, love and peace, along with those who call on the Lord out of a pure heart."

2 Timothy 2:22 (NIV)

When all is said and done, men use women, and women use men. It's a sad fact of life, but one that Christ abhors. God doesn't want us to use each other for selfish gain, even if it's mutual and consensual.

I think about that young girl now, wondering what became of her. Did she die? Was she beaten and murdered? Did she become a drug addict. I don't know and I'll never know.

Unless of course ... she committed her life to Christ. That's my wish for her, and, if she did, then I'll meet her in heaven, and only then will I find out her story.

We live in a licentious society, and not a day goes by that I'm not tempted by a billboard or an online ad, featuring a scantily clad and beautiful woman.

When that happens to you, be reminded that this woman is a creation of God, just like you and I. She has a mother and a father and sisters and brothers. She was made in the image of God, so we should act accordingly.

glory
[glawr-ee]

noun
1. very great praise, honor, or dis-
tinction bestowed by common con-
sent; renown:

de facto
[dee -fak-toh]

adverb, adjective
1. in fact; in reality.

"Blessed be the Lord, my rock,
Who trains my hands for war,
And my fingers for battle;

Psalm 144:1 (NIV)

THE GLORY OF WAR

WHEN I WAS A KID I BELIEVED war was glorious. It was a game that I played with the neighbor boys on a weekly basis. We grew up poor, so we used sticks for guns, pointing them at each other and yelling, "Bang! Bang! You're dead!" We would argue back and forth.

"I shot you first!"

"No, I shot you first!"

"No you didn't. You missed!"

We'd put walnuts in socks and use them for bombs and build forts out of logs. My father who'd been wounded in combat during the Korean War knew differently, but he seldom talked about it.

War movies seldom tell the whole truth about war. They are designed to glorify it, to make money, to reveal only a part of the truth. Movies that tell the whole truth seldom have a high degree of commercial value. Why? Because most people don't want to know the truth. Like Jack Nicholson said in the movie *A Few Good Men*: "You can't handle the truth!"

War is dirty and abhorrent. It brings out the best and the worst of humanity. This morning I watched the movie *Gettysburg* with Jeff Bridges as Colonel Chamberlain and Martin Sheen as General Robert E Lee. I've watched it many times, but ... why do I keep going back to it? My wife doesn't get it. I think it makes her wonder about me.

I think it's a lot of things. While I hate the brutality, the killing and the blood, I can't help but be moved by the process of war, by the good things it brings out in the people who fight it.

When a man throws his body on a grenade to save his fellow warriors, then I am moved to become a better person. It reminds me of Christ and what He did for us on the cross.

Greater love has no one than this: to lay down one's life for one's friends.

John 15:13 (NIV)

I believe that God hates war. I hate war. But to deny a war already in progress is foolish and suicidal. Satan attacks us on a daily basis. He attacks our church; he attacks our country; he attacks our families. All Christians are at war. It is the defacto state of all Christ followers.

Listen to Colonel Chamberlain explain why the North is fighting the South.

"If you look at history you'll see men fight for pay, or women, or some other kind of loot. They fight for land, or because a king makes them, or just because they like killing. But we're here for something new. This hasn't happened much in the history of the world. We are an army out to set other men free."

When I look back over the 20th century, with all its wars, bloodshed, tyranny and death, I can't help but see how mankind is failing. It seems that the quality of war, that the life of our young, has been cheapened and exploited by our political leaders.

The moral of the story?

MANY OF THE WARS WE FIGHT ARE AVOIDABLE; they're the product of mistakes or inaction or even weakness. Others are fought for the greedy, selfish gain of industry or politicians.

The Vietnam War was protested against, hated, scorned and excoriated by many in that time period. When these same soldiers returned from a war they never wanted to fight, they were met at the airport and spit upon and called murderers. That was wrong and misguided.

War is hell. It brings out the best and worst that humanity has to offer.

There's many a boy here today who looks on war as all glory but it is all hell.

— William Tecumseh Sherman

"All of us who served in one war or another know very well that all wars are the glory and the agony of the young."

— Gerald R. Ford

"There is no glory in war, yet from the blackness of its history, there emerge vivid colours of human character and courage. Those who risked their lives to help their friends."

— Silvia Cartwright

"The supreme art of war is to subdue the enemy without fighting."

— Sun Tzu

When all is said and done, it is tyrants and elected politicians who start wars. They hold the central reins of power; they enact the draft; they choose who will fight in their stead; while they sit in padded chairs in great halls, feasting at banquets, reaping the glory and growing rich and fat while gorging off the blood of our young.

And the 21st century isn't getting much better. But here's one important thing to remember: never confuse those who fight and die with those who lounge in the halls of power.

Respect the warrior. He chooses to fight because it's in his nature, but he doesn't choose the war itself. He just goes where he's ordered.

"a time to love and a time to hate, a time for war and a time for peace."

Ecclesiastes 3:8 (NIV)

apocalypse
[uh-pok-uh-lips]

noun
2. any of a class of Jewish or Christian writings that appeared from about 200 b.c. to a.d. 350 and were assumed to make revelations of the ultimate divine purpose.
3. a prophetic revelation, especially concerning a cataclysm in which the forces of good permanently triumph over the forces of evil.

dictionary.com

*"The revelation from Jesus Christ, which
God gave him to show his servants what
must soon take place."*

Revelation 1:1 (NIV)

THE APOCALYPSE

I WRITE APOCALYPTIC FICTION FOR A
living, and its getting tougher to do with each passing day. Why you ask? Let's look at it this way. Two
years ago I'd wake up in the morning, roll over in bed and
pick up my cell phone. I'd answer emails and check the
news just to make sure something big and bad hadn't happened while I was sleeping. I don't do that anymore.

It seems every day, without fail, something big and bad
happens in America. Violent crime is up. Social unrest ...
escalating. Global pandemic ... a way of life. In my 4-book
fiction series *The God Virus*, the power grid was brought
down by a terrorist attack. In my 3-book series *The Covid
Chronicles*, society was laid low by a second pandemic.

When I first started writing apocalyptic fiction it was
a lot of fun. But now ... not so much. What happens to
a writer when fact becomes scarier than fiction? Stephen
King must be pulling his hair out right now as he won-
ders, *How do I scare people when the things happening in*

their lives are worse than my own bizarre imagination?

I suppose the difference for me is my stories are Christian in nature. I try to infuse all my characters and plot lines with hope, encouragement and love. Forget that it's the end of the world as we know it. Don't focus on that or it'll drive you bonkers.

I feel sorry for non-Christians living in today's world when death, chaos and mayhem are all around them. The suicide rate went way up throughout the height of the first Covid pandemic. People without hope are more likely to give up and seek the ultimate end to their lives. But us Christians ... we have a hope and a promise. And not just any hope and promise ... a hope and promise from the Lord of the Universe!

But even with that, I found myself getting discouraged last year, simply because there was no end in sight. And, after a year, I began to wonder, *That light at the end of the tunnel ... is it God or a train?*

Forty-six years ago I found God in Marine Corps boot camp. Job found God in the aftermath of death, poverty and destruction of all he owned. Noah found God as he rocked on the waves of an apocalyptic flood, and Abraham found God as he raised a knife over the bound body of his young son, Isaac.

Is it possible to find God during easy and happy times? Yes, of course, and some people do that. But for most, that's not the way it works. You've heard the phrase "A fox-hole conversion." Just like an alcoholic has to bottom out before he gets help, so it is with most of us. Only when we come to the end of our rope, only then will we find God, who is waiting patiently, sitting on a rock, and wondering to Himself, *Skip, I've been sitting here on this rock for a million years ... what took you so long to find me?* I'm not sure how to answer that one. I guess I should just tell the truth and apologize. "Sorry God. I would've been here sooner, but I was busy exhausting all other possibilities."

The moral of the story?

WHEN I FIRST STARTED WRITING APOCALYPTIC FICtion it was a lot of fun, because I knew it was all in my own head and would go no further. But what happens when society teeters on the brink of collapse? When you lose your job? When you don't have enough money to pay your bills or buy food for your family?

What happens when reality rocks your faith? Remember in earlier chapters where I told of stories where I came to the end of myself, of my own strength? In retrospect, that's a good place to be. Because most people don't find God in the midst of plenty, in the midst of strength and good times. Most people find God during hardship and trial. And it's the hardship and the tough times that bring us all closer to God.

TEOTWAWKI
(The End of the World as We know it)

noun

A catastrophic event that destroys the existing institutions and norms of society.

lexico.com

It's the end of the world as we know it.
It's the end of the world as we know it.
It's the end of the world as we know it
and I feel fine.

REM Rock Band

When all is said and done, we don't like living through hard times, but it is usually the hard times that draw us closer to God. We tend to cuddle up to God when danger is all around us. "Help me, God, Save me."

God saves us and then we say "thank you, God" and then go on with our lives as though nothing bad ever happened.

I watch my chickens and they teach me a lot about humanity. The baby chicks stray from the hen during good times, but when they see the shadow of the hawk's wings pass them on the ground, they run back to Momma and hide beneath the safety of her body.

As you go through the day, try to stay beneath God's wings in all you do. It's safer there and a lot more fun!

finite
[fahy-nahyt]

adjective
1. having bounds or limits; not infinite; measurable.
2. Mathematics.
(of a set of elements) capable of being completely counted.
not infinite or infinitesimal.
not zero.
3. subject to limitations or conditions, as of space, time, circumstances, or the laws of nature:

*"8 Finally, brothers and sisters, whatever
is true, whatever is noble, whatever is right,
whatever is pure, whatever is lovely, whatever is admirable—if anything is excellent
or praiseworthy—think about such things."*

Philippians 4:8 (NIV)

BLUEBERRY PERSPECTIVE

THIS MORNING MY WIFE AND I took the kids blueberry picking at a nearby fruit farm. I didn't want to do it. I didn't have time. I had to earn the money to pay for the berries, and I certainly wouldn't do that by wasting time at a fruit farm. I needed to be working at the computer.

But my wife encouraged me to go with them ... so I did.

We were there for only about 90 minutes, but during that short hour and a half, I was reminded of some very important things in life.

Blueberry bushes are only about three to five feet tall, so it's quite easy for me to look over them and keep track of my kids. But my 10-year-old daughter is shorter than the bushes, and that reminded me of a time 55 years ago when I was just a tot. My mom would take us to this very same fruit farm and let us pick blueberries. She would then make jam and we'd use it for peanut butter and jam sandwiches throughout the year.

Sunrise Reflections: Finding Hope in Hard Times

While watching my kids pick berries this morning, my mind was transported back in time to when I was just a kid. The owner of the farm would joke about weighing us kids before and after we picked so he'd know how much we'd eaten. To be honest with you, I usually ate until I made myself sick.

On one occasion, I became separated from my mother and was running lost through the blueberry lanes yelling for her. I was terrified because I didn't know where she was, and the blueberry bushes seemed like trees, towering over my head. I felt like I was in a dark, forboding jungle. She heard me yelling and came to save me. In reality, she was just a few rows away, no more than 20 yards or so.

In my mind, I thought she was a million miles away and that I'd never see her again. But, from my mother's perspective, it was no big deal. She could see over the bushes and knew exactly where I was. In reality, I was never lost at all, because she was always watching over me. I was never in any danger.

We get that way with God sometimes. He is always there, always watching over us. He knows exactly what we're doing and what we need. But because we can't see Him, we get scared. It reminds me of Peter walking on the water.

29 "Come," he said.
Then Peter got down out of the boat, walked on the water and came toward Jesus. 30 But when he saw the wind, he was afraid and, beginning to sink, cried out, "Lord, save me!"
31 Immediately Jesus reached out his hand and caught him. "You of little faith," he said, "why did you doubt?"

Matthew 21:29-31 (NIV)

The moment Peter doubted Jesus, he sank beneath the waves.

The moral of the story?

IN ORDER TO SUCCESSFULLY WALK ON WATER, PETER needed a different perspective, one not hampered by time and space. When we take our eyes off the most important things in life, we flounder and drown. Life is dangerous to be sure, but we are not without a champion who watches over us and protects us. Jesus is our protector and defender. And, if we ask Him to, He'll reach out His hand and pull us up from beneath the deadly waves.

As you go through your day, as the world seeks to wear you down, keep your eyes on God, your protector and defender. Think on good things.

"We can complain because rose bushes have thorns, or rejoice because thorns have roses."

   – Alphonse Karr, A Tour Round My Garden

"It is the obvious which is so difficult to see most of the time. People say 'It's as plain as the nose on your face.' But how much of the nose on your face can you see, unless someone holds a mirror up to you?"

   – Isaac Asimov, I, Robot

"Charles Wallace and the unicorn moved through the time-spinning reaches of a far glazy, and he realized that the galaxy itself was part of a mighty orchestra, and each star and planet within the galaxy added its own instrument to the music of the spheres. As long as the ancient harmonies were sung, the universe would not entirely lose its joy."

   – Madeleine L'Engle, A Swiftly Tilting Planet

When all is said and done, God's perspective is different than our own. We see our lives through the limited view of finite man. God sees our lives from outside the bonds of space and time. We see ourselves only from the inside looking out.

God is unique in that He can view every aspect of our lives either from a million miles away, or, He can zoom in closer and analyze every molecule of our body. Maybe that's why He's so much smarter than we are, and why we should trust His view of things instead of our own.

mistake
[mi-steyk]

noun
1. an error in action, calculation, opinion, or judgment caused by poor reasoning, carelessness, insufficient knowledge, etc.

"2 We all stumble in many ways. Anyone who is never at fault in what they say is perfect, able to keep their whole body in check."

James 3:2 (NIV)

SECOND WIND

BECAUSE OF THE MANY MISTAKES I've made in my life, I have 7 children from three different women. Go ahead ... let that sink in for a minute or two and then start reading again. To those of you who've been married to the same woman for your entire lives, then my hat's off to you and I genuflect my entire body with all the enthusiasm of a freak show contortionist.

Now, don't misunderstand my meaning. I don't mean to say I regret my mistakes. No, to the contrary. I value them. I revere them, and I know in my heart of hearts that I am but the sum total of all my mistakes as well as good choices. Perhaps, just perhaps, if I were to eliminate my mistakes, I wouldn't have become the person I am today. Indeed, I believe that with all my heart.

One very important thing I've learned to do over the years, is to laugh at myself. No matter what I do, no matter how bad I screw up, inevitably, down the road, I'll find myself laughing at my own foolishness. It's a coping mechanism I suppose, but it also helps me to maintain my sanity, especially while in the midst of pain and suffering. Many times, while still in the throes of all my self-inflicted agony and remorse, I hear myself say in the empty chasms of my mind, "Wow, Skip. That was really stupid!" And then I laugh and go on with life.

But one thing I can't laugh at is the way some of my own mistakes have affected the people I love. To be sure, my own children were hurt because of mistakes I've made. On the other hand, many of my children were the natural by-product of my poor life decisions. Without my mistakes, my children would never have been born.

I just finished watching a movie called *Peggy Sue Got Married*. In the movie, Peggy Sue, played by Kathleen Turner, attends her 25th high school reunion and ends up going back in time to her high school days. She is determined not to make the same mistakes, and tries desperately to do better the second time around.

Towards the end of the movie, she visits her grandpa and asks him this question:

Peggy Sue: If you could do it all again,
Grandpa. What would you do different?

Grandpa: I'd have taken better care of my teeth.

I think what grandpa meant was this: "I have no regrets." At the end of the movie, Peggy Sue returns to her original place in time and reunites with her husband, even though she'd long believed that marrying him was the biggest mistake of her life.

I agree with Peggy Sue and her grandpa. When I look back over my life, I see a multitude of mistakes; things I did poorly; things I shouldn't have said or done, but ... in the end, I have no regrets.

The moral of the story?

I AM MARRIED TO THE MOST WONDERFUL WOMAN ON the planet. Sara has helped me through some pretty tough times. When we met, I was a single dad, twice divorced, and trying to raise two young children while their mother was in hospice dying of cancer.

Today, when I ask Sara what she likes about me and why she agreed to marry me, she always says: "Through all your pain and hard times, I like the person you've become. The way you responded to your mistakes, filled you with strength and compassion."

Here's the bottom line. If I could go back in time and do it all over again, I'd make the same mistakes in order to get the same results. I like the person I've become, the person that God has made me. My life is so happy now, but if I'd never been forced to grow through all my mistakes, then Sara wouldn't have been attracted to me.

Embrace your mistakes and make peace with them. Oh, and one other thing: take better care of your teeth.

"You're having a hard time and lately you don't feel so good

You're getting a bad reputation in your neighborhood

It's alright, it's alright

Sometimes that's what it takes

You're only human, you're allowed to make your share of mistakes"

– Billy Joel
(from "You're Only Human-Second Wind")

When all is said and done, I am the sum total of all my words, deeds and actions. To change my history, is to change who I am. While I've made some huge, life-changing mistakes, errors that have caused myself and the ones I love great pain ... I wouldn't go back in time and do it over again in an attempt to fix it. I would probably just muck it up even worse.

God gives us only one first chance. That's when we make most of our mistakes. Then we learn from it and He gives us another chance, and another, and another, and another. And life goes on.

But to go back in time to try and make it right is a mistake ... perhaps the biggest mistake of all.

worship
[wur-ship]

noun
1. reverent honor and homage paid to God or a sacred personage, or to any object regarded as sacred.

dictionary.com

potluck

noun
1. food or a meal that happens to be available without special preparation
2. Also called potluck supper, pot-luck dinner, potluck lunch . a meal, especially for a large group, to which participants bring various foods to be shared.

dictionary.com

"24 God is spirit, and his worshipers must worship in the Spirit and in truth."

– John 4:24 (NIV)

TREE WORSHIP

PEOPLE WORSHIP GOD IN A LOT of different ways. Perhaps there are as many worship styles as there are people. Some people like to raise up their hands and hover and vibrate, while others simply bow their heads in reverence and awe. I've seen people roll down aisles like tumbleweeds, and I've seen them speak in tongues, and fall down on the ground slain in the spirit.

Some people dance. Some people sing. Some fast before worship and others have a feast afterwards. I think some of the best food I've had in my life is after a church worship service.

I've heard it said that Baptists have but three holy sacraments: communion, marriage and potluck dinners. I grew up in a Baptist church, and we'd have something called a potluck dinner once a month. As a kid, I lived for that dinner. I would fill my plate to the brim, wolf it all down, and then go back for seconds, and thirds and sometimes even fourths. Thinking back, I still yearn for those days of my youth and eating with impunity.

Last week we visited a different kind of church. It was an Orthodox church that was completely liturgical. It was a bit freaky for me, all the chanting and repetition; it was enough to make a Baptist boy cower in his pew. (Except they didn't have pews, and most people either stood, sat on blankets or stadium chairs.) The priest was dressed up in fancy robes and he walked around the room shaking a metal container filled with burning incense. I know everything they did has biblical roots and some symbolic significance, but I have no idea what it is. My wife was loving it, but it was a bit much for me, so I was content simply to respectfully gawk.

About twenty minutes into the service, I got up and walked out. It wasn't out of disrespect or lack of interest; it was the incense. For some reason it was making me dizzy, and I needed some fresh air. I walked outside, and when the fresh air hit me, I smiled. Then I looked to the left of the parking lot and saw a sign that said "hiking trail." I walked over and saw a well-groomed path leading into the woods. I walked down the path and into the woods. I listened to the birds, saw the sun filtering down through the leaves where it hit the forest floor.

I walked until I came to an apple tree of some sort. They were weird-looking apples, but I took a bite anyway, before spitting it out onto the ground. It was sour.

And then the oddest thing happened. I started talking out loud to God. I said, "Wow, God. This is great! You did a really good job here. Thanks for making all this."

And then I realized that my worship language is centered on God's creation. Every fall I go into the woods deer hunting. I climb up 20 feet into a treestand, sit down in full camo with either a bow or a gun, and I worship God for hours at a time.

I've shared that with my wife, but I'm not sure she buys my story. She thinks I just love to hunt.

The moral of the story?

I DON'T BELIEVE THERE IS JUST ONE GOD-ACCEPTED way to worship. I've been to churches where they thought an electric guitar was from the devil, and I've been to churches where the music was so loud I needed hearing protection. Is it possible that both extremes are acceptable and pleasing to God?

I walked back down the hiking trail back to the church, leaving God's creation behind. I went back into the building and sat beside my wife and kids. I tried my best to listen to the liturgy, but it just wasn't me.

My body was inside a brick building ... but my heart was in the woods.

"The most valuable thing the Psalms do for me is to express the same delight in God which made David dance."

— *C.S. Lewis*

"We must never rest until everything inside us worships God."

— *A. W. Tozer*

"Worship is our response to the overtures of love from the heart of the Father."

— *Richard J. Foster*

Therefore, since we are receiving a kingdom that cannot be shaken, let us be thankful, and so worship God acceptably with reverence and awe, for our "God is a consuming fire."

Hebrews 12:28 (NIV)

When all is said and done, we worship God wherever we are. The apostle Paul worshiped in prison, while making tents, in synagogues and while traveling from one city to another.

In the final analysis, I think worship has less to do with beautiful, expensive buildings, and more to do with the beauty of our heart and soul.

We worship in spirit and in truth. My spirit soars 20 feet off the ground in a tree. When I look out over the woods; when I hear the hoot of an owl or the coo of a mourning dove, and hear and feel the handiwork of God.

I feel closer to God in a tree than I ever could in a building made of brick and mortar, surrounded by pavement. That's just me, but I think God made me this way for a reason.

legacy
[leg-uh-see]

noun
2. anything handed down from the past, as from an ancestor or predecessor:

*"And she added, "Who would have said to
Abraham that Sarah would nurse children?
Yet I have borne him a son in his old age.""*

Genesis 21:7 (NIV)

THE LEGACY

MY LIFE IS WONDERFULLY
strange right now, though it's different from
that of most of my friends. I grew up with
most of them; we went to the same school or college, or
worked together for decades. Most of them are retiring
now, having served their lives in the corporate world or
education or whatever other career choice that suited
them. Some of them winter in Florida and spend the
warm months up here in the frozen north woods. Others
immerse themselves into their grandkids, making whatever investment they can, enjoying their golden years and
passing on what wisdom they can to the next generation.
Still others just live out what's left of their lives mowing
their lawn too much and yelling at the neighbor kids who
walk on their dead grass.

But my life isn't like that ... not even a little bit.

Even though I'm eligible to draw a monthly social se-
curity check, I choose not to. I'm just going to keep on

working, writing, teaching, doing radio shows and podcasts. It's what I love. And here's the thing, when I was in the corporate world, most of my friends talked incessantly about retirement; what they were going to do; where they would travel, and how they would spend their golden years. It was like they were tolerating their youth and middle age just so they could reach retirement and finally do all the things they really wanted to do.

Here's what I'm finding. Some of them die early and leave a spouse behind. Sure, she has a lot of money now, and can travel whereever she wants, but ... she's all alone. Some of the workaholics get bored and go back to work, usually for a fraction of what they're accustomed to. But they don't care; at least they feel useful again.

Me? I'm never going to retire. I don't want to. I'm living my dream. And I have the kind of job that becomes better with age and experience. Sure, I could end up with dementia or one day forget my name, but ... if that happens, well then ... ignorance is bliss.

While all my friends are slowing down, my life is speeding up. Sara and I have been married for 17 years now, and we have three children, ages 15, 11 and 10. Even though I'm 64 years old, I'm so wrapped up in raising children, that I have no time for retirement or other such nonsense that old people are accustomed to.

Do you remember that old advertisement for Clairol beauty products? It always featured a beautiful, middle-aged woman, who looked only 25, shaking her voluptuous mane of hair back and forth in slow motion. And the voice-over would say "You're not getting older ... You're getting better!"

It's a commercial, so it doesn't have to be true; it just has to appeal to the customer and make you buy the product.

The moral of the story?

Y͟OU ARE DEFINITELY GETTING OLDER. ALL OF US are, but think about it and be honest. Are you getting better or are you just getting older? And I'm not talking about your body ... I'm talking about your soul. It's a given that my body is but a shadow of its former self.

Here's what I've learned as I raise my third litter of kids: in some ways it's tougher being a parent at age 64 than it was at age 28. At 28 I could stay up all night with a crying baby and still make it through the next workday. I could work 12 hours, then come home and teach my son how to play ball or take them out for ice cream. But here's the bad part: I was ignorant, and I had no idea how to parent, so my first batch of kids got the short end of the stick in that regard. Many times I just guessed at what the right thing to do really was.

Now, raising kids at age 64, I have the opposite problem. I have tons of wisdom, comparatively speaking, and I know which mistakes to avoid. I know what to do and what not to do. I have a lot of experience on the job, and my present batch of kids benefits from that. I just wish I had more energy. I recall another decades-old commercial for a pain reliever. The announcer said, "Tie a bow? Simple. Except when arthritis flares up."

Now, before I play ball with my kids, I take a thousand milligrams of ibuprofen as a preemptive strike.

"The greatest legacy one can pass on to one's children and grandchildren is not money or other material things accumulated in one's life, but rather a legacy of character and faith."

– Billy Graham

"What you leave behind is not what is engraved in stone monuments, but what is woven into the lives of others."

– Pericles

"The greatest legacy we can leave our children is happy memories."

– Og Mandino

When all is said and done, I'm a better parent now than I used to be. Even though my body has seen better days, my heart has gained some measure of wisdom, patience and a sense of what children need.

Hard times are here, and times are getting worse. I often wonder: what do my kids need from me? A lot of obvious things come to mind right away: wisdom, love, discipline, truth and a host of others. I give my kids all those things as best I can, but, along with that, I try to give them happy experiences they'll be able to remember when I'm gone.

Part of my job is to give my kids memories that will sustain them for the next 50 years, because when life gets tough and times are hard, then, it's the good times we look back on that give us the strength to go on. I'm trying my best to give my kids a legacy of memories that will last a lifetime.

35 Heaven and earth will pass away, but my words will never pass away.

Matthew 24:35 (NIV)

In Closing

I'M SITTING IN MY TRUCK NOW, parked on the small bridge of the creek that runs through the heart of our property. I'm listening to the water bounce off the rocks as it flows on by. A few hundred yards north, it will flow onto the neighbor's property, then join with another small creek and continue on down to ... well, I don't know where. The end of the creek lies beyond my sight.

But I take the creek on faith. Even though I can't see its end, I know that is has an end. As I said earlier: everything with a beginning ... has an ending.

This creek is my respite, a tiny arbor, a place of peace where I rest from the troubles of this world. God made the creek ... and God made me. I find comfort in that.

Even though we live in a fallen world, one filled with pain and suffering, torture and death, injustice and pain ... we also live in a world of unsurpassed beauty and joy. We see joy all around us: in the faces of young children, in the eyes of a young mother who's just given birth; in the face of a young man who's just fallen in love. Joy is evident for those who seek it.

But it seems that the longer I live, the more difficult it is to find that joy, and that is a sadness indeed.

Perhaps I need to live more by faith and less by sight. I believe that joy, like love, is a choice. Just as I choose to live for God, so also can I choose to be happy.

> *11 I am not saying this because I am in need, for I have learned to be content whatever the circumstances. 12 I know what it is to be in need, and I know what it is to have plenty. I have learned the secret of being content in any and every situation, whether well fed or hungry, whether living in plenty or in want. 13 I can do all this through him who gives me strength.*
>
> *Philippians 4:11-13 (NIV)*

Like Paul, I am learning to be content in a fallen world. I think maybe, part of the secret is looking on the bright side. That would be ... the sunrise. It happens every morning without fail. It happened yesterday and it will happen tomorrow as well. We don't even have to do anything to earn it. It's God's eternal gift to humanity. Just because ... He loves us.

I know you are in hard times right now. We all are. . You are in pain, no worse than that; you are in agony. Perhaps your spouse left you for someone else. Perhaps your son or daughter just died. Maybe you are in prison and feel no hope for the future, that God can never forgive you for the bad things you've done.

But none of us have to go it alone. God is there, holding your hand, reassuring you, whispering in your ear: "Don't worry little one. Trust me. I've got this."

I mean ... think about it from His perspective. God has seen worse. He was alone, bleeding on the cross, dying in pain and agony, but, still ... He made it through just fine. And so will you. Just don't give up. Never give up and never give in.

Always remember. Everything with a beginning ... has an ending. And that is a very comforting thought in the midst of hard times.

So, as I get ready to close out this book, I look down at the creek, at the sun on the water as it reflects and flows on by; and I remind myself that hope springs eternal, because all hope stems from God.

Rest now in God's arms ... in hope, in faith and in love.

8 Finally, brothers and sisters, whatever is true, whatever is noble, whatever is right, whatever is pure, whatever is lovely, whatever is admirable—if anything is excellent or praiseworthy— think about such things.

Philippians 4:8 (NIV)

The creek flows by me now. Birds sing in the distance. The leaves rustle in the breeze. All these things are beautiful and a comfort to me, but ... these things can pass away. But one thing will never pass away ... God loves me ... and therein lies my hope.

Skip Coryell lives with his wife and children in Michigan. He works full time as a professional writer, and *Sunrise Reflections* is his 19th published book. He is an avid hunter and sportsman, a Marine Corps veteran, and a graduate of Cornerstone University. You can listen to Skip as he co-hosts the syndicated military talk radio show *Frontlines of Freedom* on frontlinesoffreedom.com. You can also hear his weekly podcast *The Home Defense Show* at homedefenseshow.com.

For more details on Skip Coryell, or to contact him personally, go to his website at skipcoryell.com

Books by Skip Coryell

We Hold These Truths
Bond of Unseen Blood
Church and State
Blood in the Streets
Laughter and Tears
RKBA: Defending the Right to Keep and Bear Arms
Stalking Natalie
The God Virus
The Shadow Militia
The Saracen Tide
The Blind Man's Rage
Civilian Combat - The Concealed Carry Book
Jackpine Strong
Concealed Carry for Christians
The Covid Chronicles: Surviving the Upgrade
The Covid Chronicles: Surviving the Apocalypse
The Covid Chronicles: Surviving the Solstice
The Mad American - Judgment Day
Sunrise Reflections: Finding Hope in Hard Times

This is 4 books in one! The complete 4-book God Virus apocalyptic adventure series beneath one cover. Suddenly, the lights went out, not just in one town or village, but all across the world. It was an act of cyber terrorism that plunged the world into the heart of darkness, into the 1000-year night, letting loose the demons of a billion souls, pitting dark against light, causing each person everywhere to choose sides. Not since Stephen King's "The Stand" has there been an apocalyptic thriller of such epic proportions. Read the entire 4-book series and see what happens when society's thin veneer of civility is stripped away. "The God Virus" series is gripping, seething and oozing with the best and worst humanity has to offer.

SKIP CORYELL

CONCEALED CARRY *for* **CHRISTIANS**

I started carrying a pistol almost 20 years ago, and I've been a member of a church safety team for about 15 years now. The church safety team is like other ministries in that we are serving the body of Christ, but there is one very distinct and important difference. It might get you killed.

I've been a Sunday school teacher, even Sunday School Superintendent. I've served on musical teams. I've been an usher. I've even helped in the children's ministry where they expected me to dance up and down to silly songs while making ridiculous hand motions. (Thank God there are no existing pictures for that one. It wasn't pretty.)

However, none of those jobs ever required me to take a bullet for the flock. As a Sunday School teacher, I was never expected to run towards gunshots while drawing my firearm. Most Sunday School teachers don't carry pepper spray; they don't practice open-handed skills to become proficient at taking a man to the ground and putting him in zip ties. They are not trained in the subtle arts of interrogation and visually identifying physical threats, like who is armed and who is not.

It's a different kind of ministry, requiring a different kind of Christian. However, all these concerns are not restricted to the church safety team, because they apply to any Christian who decides to carry a gun.

If you are considering carrying a gun or joining a church safety team, then, this book is a must-listen for you. You should not go into the job lightly, as there are many things to consider. Can you take a human life? Killing a fellow human being is not and should not be a natural and easy thing to do. It should be tough. It may take years of prayer and study and self-reflection before you decide the answer. Do you want to carry a gun? It's a nuisance, a total life change, and a bona fide pain in the butt. Carrying a gun dictates every facet of your life: how you treat others, what you wear, how you talk, and how you walk. It's not for everyone.

Are you willing to die to protect the ones you love? How about strangers? Will you die to protect someone you haven't even met yet. Are you willing to spend lots of time and money on training and equipment? Less than one percent of the concealed carry population ever go on to take training that is not required by the government. That statistic should scare you.

Buying a gun doesn't make you a gun fighter any more than buying a guitar makes you a rock star. We are called by God to excellence in everything we do. The gun is a powerful tool. The sacrifice you make could be supreme. It is a life-or-death decision. This book was written to empower and encourage Christians who decide to carry concealed. You are an elite corps of individuals. You are warriors. Welcome to the club! - Skip Coryell

If masculinity is toxic, then Jack Ruger is the cultural equivalent of a raging bull on steroids. Born and raised in the cold and frozen northern paradise of Michigan's upper peninsula, Chief of Police Jack Ruger is sworn to protect and defend the citizens of Jackpine. So when escaped killer Bobby Lee Harper descends on the town, threatening to kill him and all he holds dear, it's a formal declaration of war, and only one man will survive.

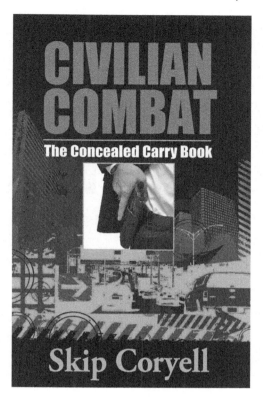

More and more people across the country are seeing the dangers in society and deciding to carry concealed to protect themselves and their families. Skip's book lays it out step by step, teaching you how to protect and defend the ones you love. Read his book and get the benefit of his 19 years of teaching experience and his lifetime of training for this important role in society. *Civilian Combat* is also a great teaching tool for other concealed carry instructors as well. It's a complete curriculum with a final test as well as important points to remember and a list of excellent resources in your journey to personal and family protection.

Skip is the creator and host of *The Home Defense Show*, a weekly 1-hour podcast about all things home, family and personal defense.

The Home Defense Show podcast is now available on iTunes, Google Play, Spreaker and Sticher. You can also find it on my YouTube channel. This should make it easier than ever for you to listen to my sweet angelic voice coming to you from deep inside the bowels of a great big empty. Don't forget to subscribe.

For more info go to homedefenseshow.com

FRONTLINES OF FREEDOM RADIO

You can hear authors Denny Gillem and Skip Coryell on one of your local stations on the number 1 military talk show in America. *Frontlines of Freedom* is syndicated on over 180 stations, and is also available as a podcast on frontlinesoffreedom.com.